Shine on
Swansea City

Shine on Swansea City 2011/12

A SEASON IN THE SUN

KEITH HAYNES

For Sarah & Victoria

Victory is sweetest when you've known defeat.
Malcolm S. Forbes
19 August 1919 – 24 February 1990

Follow the Swans every day at www.scfc2.co.uk

First published 2012

The History Press
The Mill, Brimscombe Port
Stroud, Gloucestershire, GL5 2QG
www.thehistorypress.co.uk

British Library Cataloguing in Publication Data.
A catalogue record for this book is available from the British Library.

ISBN 978 0 7524 86253
Typesetting and origination by The History Press
Printed in Great Britain

Contents

Foreword

by Leigh Dineen, Vice Chairman of Swansea City AFC

S upporting a football team is as much about the memories as it is about the present. We all have our favourite goal, our favourite match and our heroes. We remember teams that played with some finesse, others that used hard graft to gain their victories. Football also helps us remember our own history and allows us to identify with episodes in our own lives.

I started my Swansea career at about the age of eight; I went with my grandfather while on school half-term in Swansea. Now my parents lived in India, so getting to games presented a bit of an issue and my school was in Bristol, so I had my own identity. I used to wear Swansea patches on my denims back then. I am not too sure if there were many Swans fans in the area at that time! As I got older I took my place, albeit sporadically, on the North Bank, and went to games in London and in my teens and early twenties developed a real love for Swansea City. My family worked abroad as I said, so the BBC World Service was my Swansea lifeline – ear to the radio listening to games in countries like Nigeria, Sudan and Yemen. The radio dial was my only sanctuary as the newspapers sometimes took a week to arrive . . . none of the instant methods of communication that we have today.

I must have been twenty-three when I eventually came back to Swansea. My standing place at that time was the East Terrace at the Vetch Field, just above the crossbar. I was an avid Swans fan and season ticket-holder. These were the days of the Bonymaen boys – some real characters were there and great laughs were had.

By the time the new century kicked in, I was thirty-six. I was an occupier of the Centre Stand, three rows up from the directors' box, bang on the centre line: yes, I had travelled the ground clockwise. Back then the kids came with me as well, they too ready for their Swansea City journey. There used to be the odd shout in protest, as some of you well know, the managers and directors, owners and all weren't that happy with all that – some got very upset – but then again none of them were doing their jobs properly, were they?

It was then that things changed for me. I didn't set out for it to do so, it just seemed to happen. I was still a supporter but now I could have some effect on the way we did things. I joined a group of like-minded people who just wanted the best for Swansea City FC – nothing else, no hidden agendas. To say we were frightened of what lay ahead is an understatement. We knew, however, that there was no alternative and that we just had to use common sense in running the club . . . something which was in short supply elsewhere throughout football at the time. This coming together I never dreamed would lead to anything as special as what we have witnessed in recent times.

What happened in 2002 is now well documented. The Trust had been formed in 2001, born out of a growing feeling that in the not-too-distant future we would be requiring some sort of fans' group to help the club. It was at this time that Keith and I met, although we had spent many an hour on internet forums discussing and documenting the precarious position the club was in. The Trust was required even earlier than any of us envisaged and eventually took its place as part of a new consortium. I had the privilege of not only chairing the Trust but of representing it on the newly formed board. People should never underestimate the role the Trust played in the early years. Not just the fact it represented the supporter but the fact it gave the other consortium members the confidence to push forward in the knowledge that the supporters were fully behind what they were doing. If it was to fail, then it would do so trying its best for Swansea City.

The rest, as they say, is history. Ten years on and the club stands proudly as the eleventh-best team in the English pyramid. It has been achieved without vast investment, without debt, and importantly, without losing its links to the community. If we can keep that recipe, continue to involve the supporters as we go along and not lose sight of what makes being a Swansea City supporter special, then the future's a bright one for us all. I know that each and every member of the current board sees their position as a privileged one and we are all very proud to be able to represent the club.

Although it is a surprise, I have to say it is a pleasure to write this foreword. After all, Keith and I haven't locked horns on the internet for many a year. Having read *Swansea City 2010/11: Walking on Sunshine,* I had no hesitation in taking up the offer. For those who haven't read it yet, I suggest you do so as it will give you a different insight into our incredible journey.

Keith writes it as he sees it and feels it and certainly in a way that makes us wonder what's coming next! The 2011/12 season has been fantastic for everybody associated with our club. The city has seen fantastic exposure throughout the world and our great support has gained plaudits wherever we have gone. Keith will, without doubt put his own slant on it and capture moments that will live on in our memories forever. I'm sure you will all thoroughly enjoy his account of Swansea City's inaugural season in the Premier League. After all, we played and supported and sang in our own unique Swansea City way and without doubt Keith will write it in his.

Leigh Dineen, June 2012

About the Author

Keith Haynes has been writing football books for fifteen years. Now based in Gloucester, he has followed Swansea City since his first game at the Vetch Field in 1968. From the football fanzines of the early 1990s to magazines like *FourFourTwo*, tabloids, broadsheets and radio, Keith has worked tirelessly writing and broadcasting his own view of his club's fortunes.

During the 1990s he formed and co-ordinated the Swans supporters' club in the south-west of England with a membership of over three hundred – and this at a time when fortunes for the club were not as good as today. The supporters' club ran trips to games and competed in various local football leagues for fifteen years. Running end-of-season dinners with such esteemed guests as Jan Molby, friendships were formed which have remained solid and sound to this day. Now the remnants of the supporters' group watch proudly from the Swansea East Stand. Keith and the main supporters' group leaders became the central protagonists in the late 1990s as a succession of poorly prepared and thoughtless owners came in and out of Swansea City FC. They were met with a solid wall of protest every time the club was abused and cheated. In 2000 and 2001 meetings and demonstrations were arranged away from and at games to protest at the disgraceful way the club was being run both on and off the pitch. This resulted in supporters coming together from across the UK and abroad and eventually led to the now well-documented meeting in Bristol which was the catalyst for the new foundations we see today at Swansea City. Keith chose to support wholeheartedly this new trust and today enjoys very much the successes that saw overthrown every questionable owner of Swansea City for five years.

It took a lot of effort, hard work and time to educate many supporters, who in the end took to the streets in their thousands to save the club and take a form of action so direct it surfaced in the supporters' trust and board we have today at Swansea City – it should be a template for any club in any league of the football pyramid.

Today the club sits proudly within football's elite, a story so remarkable it is unlikely to be repeated anywhere ever again – but what a story.

Away from football Keith is very much involved in music and through his band and record label has enjoyed remarkable success himself, a story not for these pages but a story all the same. Nowadays there is no need to protest and demonstrate to save what is dear or to keep alive what is loved and cherished, just a desire to support and enjoy every moment of this wonderful club's football journey – Wales' premier football club, Swansea City.

Follow Keith on twitter @_KeithHaynes

Author's Note

This book has been written as the first season of Premier League football is undertaken by Wales' premier football team, Swansea City. It comes with the emotion you feel after defeat and victory, it is written as the story unfurls. This means that words are chosen in the cathartic release of the moment. A retrospective work of this kind doesn't carry the passion that is felt as a fan writing a biographical account that will be a part of history forever. It just wouldn't work. What you read is what I felt throughout a traumatic sporting season, the words are at times carefully picked, and in others maybe you need to leave well alone. The words 'hate' and 'love' will be used, and should only be taken in the context of football, as should the damning attacks I make at times on the British press. Yes, maybe I should insert a smiley here. When you write from the heart, you bleed all your emotions on to the pages. That's the way it is as a football fan so passionate about your team. If it's not for you I will understand, but take a while to see if it is. A football journey, no matter who writes it and who they follow, is always worthy of a few moments of anyone's time.

And this football journey is a very special one indeed.

Acknowledgements

My personal thanks have to go to my many friends and colleagues, contacts and supporters of Swansea City FC. Without doubt my family deserve special thanks and to them I offer my sincere gratitude for your continued support of my bizarre life and projects. To Jon Wilsher at Swansea City; Leigh Dineen; Alan Curtis; Colin Pascoe; Phil at Planet Swans and Jim White at scfc2.co.uk; my secret contacts and field mice who talk to me in the middle of the night; all my new Twitter friends and enemies; the staff at Gloucester Royal Hospital who ensured I finished this book; Michelle and all at The History Press for their faith in me as an author and writer and most of all you, the person who has been on my previous journeys and now comes along again as we ride on the crest of a white swan one more time. Cheers y'all, the Swansea express is ready to depart, all aboard!

Up front with
Keith Haynes

As the 2010/11 football season concluded at Wembley Stadium on Monday 30 May 2011, 44,000 Swansea City supporters made their way home to the far-flung corners of the globe. At this point some pretty poignant statements were made by the media, press and certain fans of other clubs. 'Swansea City are the first Welsh football club to play in the Premier League' was one. That's a fair shout, if not obvious. 'The biggest away following for the club in its ninety-nine-year history,' was another. OK, that happens to most clubs when they play at Wembley. And here is my favourite, 'The club will be relegated by Christmas with the fewest points ever, and set a Premier League record.' Oh – cheers for that, and Saturday's lottery numbers will be . . . . I even found time to laugh out loud about an Elvis quote – apparently finding him alive is more of a possibility than Swansea City staying in the Premier League after one season.

We have heard all this before; the very negative side of success once again being our companion. And all before my weary but happy companions had left the London suburbs on our way back to the south-west of England. Throughout this coming season there would be many, many absurd, ill-thought-out and pretty provocative additions to this initial outburst, and indeed some prophetic, sympathetic and very passionate thoughts as well. Supporters and media all wanting to chip in with their ten pence worth of views. The fans, for me, deserve their sentiments; these are the people who follow and support their teams, be they from Wales' premier football club Swansea City or the lesser clubs like Cardiff, West Ham, Birmingham City, Nottingham Forest, Reading, the Sheffield two, Leeds United and many more. I jest with you slightly, of course, but you would feel the same way as I did that rainy, blustery day as we left the smoke for more healthy surroundings. We are a Premier League football club, unlike those I have just mentioned, at least for now, and that's good enough for me.

We were so happy, so, so blissfully happy. I find it hard to believe that my club had made it so far in such a short space of time. Going over old ground now about how we got here, and the war that was fought and won is not right: that has been covered in *Swansea City 2010/11: Walking on Sunshine*, and you, dear reader, will have to set about getting that account of the club's promotion campaign to the Premier League to read for yourself if you want to catch up on Swansea City's recent past, especially you newbies to the 'Jack Army'. I thoroughly recommend it. Of course I will harp back at times, but you won't get the full fighting picture here. My last book set the scene for this very favourable and testing book which I set about writing the day after we returned from Wembley.

I will be honest here and now, other publishers were interested in hearing from me, and wanted dearly to have my wet signature on a publishing contract to move away from my current deal. And this made me think. Quite a lot. Not so much about my loyalty, but loyalty in general.

There are players, like supporters, who want the best deal for themselves as they travel on their football journey. These players want the best money, the best contract and the fans want the best prices, and the best effort. I just wanted to work with someone (not anyone) like my current publishers who (after a little time) actually supported my efforts, and who could take the time to talk to me, explain to me, and understand me. They won the day. In sales terms *Swansea City 2010/11: Walking on Sunshine* far exceeded expectations. Usually you write a book and it sells a few hundred, maybe a few thousand copies, and this has been my recent experience, but my last account astounded me. Not only did it sell in its thousands, and had a number of reprints, it sold throughout the world as well. It enabled me to set aside time to write about this season that has passed: the 2011/12 Premier League season. It didn't reward me with jewels and houses, but it did make sure I had enough finance in place to put into this book more time, energy and, if it can be bought in monetary terms, passion. I'm not a football player, so you can be the judge on that last statement.

Setting out on this journey, our first Premier League journey (but of course not our first top-flight journey), held little fear for me to complete in detail as favourably as my last book. What concerned me was the amount of press talk there was on Swansea City, not just the incorrect statements on our recent history, players' names, or lack of knowledge on who runs the club, but maybe, our ability to actually ride this storm out and stay in the Premier League. Yes, all the pretty alarming negativity piling in from the Fleet Street know-alls was beginning to make an impact on me. I was beginning to believe them. I thought about Derby County and how badly they performed when Paul Jewell was their manager, and how pathetic they looked at the foot of the division. Relegated by December almost. Would that be us? Would we travel here and there being beaten by six, seven, eight goals a game by Manchester United, Liverpool, Chelsea, Arsenal, Tottenham and all? Would we indeed even match up to Wigan, Bolton and Wolves? After all they are established, well-paid and extremely rich football clubs in comparison to Swansea City. The £90m windfall the club will receive over time would have to be well managed, and that never guarantees you safety. Look at the many clubs who have failed after trying to buy success, they are too numerous to mention. Would that be us? Those journalists like Martin Lipton, John Cross and even the *Western Mail*'s Cardiff-based scribes have a lot of expertise following football, and they see things (apparently) that we don't as they are expert commentators of British football. This is a football journo fact. The likes of Paul Abbandanato at the *Western Mail* have years and years of experience, so what he sees, I should see too. The new football editors at the *Guardian* and the *Daily Mail*, the *Sun*, the *Mirror*, the *Star* and *Independent* have much to say and their coverage at times is considered the world's best journalism, so they must understand the game far better than you or I. This is fact, I am not being sarcastic when I say this.

I mention now all these respected broadsheets and tabloids because these are the million-a-day sellers which carry the football stories of today; they comment on football and more specifically Premier League football day in and day out. They have avenues of exploration in to clubs that none of us have. They have contacts on contacts, and the telephone numbers of all the right agents and all the right players. All we have as fans is our judgement, our belief and our untainted and undamaged hope. Swansea City has been catapulted from League 2 and oblivion to the very top of the world football ladder. Now everyone wants to know us and write about us. A part of the world's most-watched, most-talked-about and most-envied league, the club are no longer just a football team in Wales, fighting for survival like our neighbours Cardiff City. They are now at the top of their game – the country's (Wales') finest football side. They carry with them the hope of every football neutral in Wales now, not just the many thousands of Swansea City fans. With Premier League football comes Premier League fans – the glory-hunter stalking the outer echelons of football fandom, looking for success and demanding million-pound players for the reserves. I think they will be disappointed as modern-day Swansea City supporters. These things don't happen here, regardless of the league we play in. However, there is a complete package, the merchandise, the look, the prospects, the feel, the colours, the glory and the being involved. These all attract the football fan. Commercially the club will make millions from the Premier League, have no fear. The club will make millions from worldwide exposure and the club will make millions from television deals both here and abroad. And because of that they will have to spend millions too.

The club's budget will already be at the forefront of the board's thinking and especially the Chairman, Huw Jenkins. He has sacrificed much to be at the helm of this club and he deserves a brief moment of reflective glory as well. This glory won't last long though – as quickly as the plaudits are dealt, the sharks will circle. The press love a sacrificial lamb, and with the sheep stock looking good in the Principality they won't think twice about slaughtering Swansea and its football team if they must. There are stories to write and readers to please. They are not beholden to the Liberty Stadium – if the club are looking like they are going down, the knives will be out very quickly indeed. The press won't be returning here too quickly if the Swans display what everybody expects, and that's nothing at all. It's not as if they have to be careful what they write about our club – we are not Arsenal – the press write column inches from air-conditioned offices in London, and we as a club to them mean nothing at all. They won't care if they are not welcome at Swansea, but they would do if we were Manchester United, so the vicious prose could come quite quickly. Beholden to no one are the British press, unless of course you're established. Then they will think what they write before going to print. This is frightening.

Kudos comes in many forms, some people are happy to be recognised, and flirted with for a brief period by the media and the financial rewards mean little. Seekers of fame with no talent appear very briefly before your eyes most days and weeks. Fame indeed. You can be famous now without any talent at all – this is the British way in 2012. In fact most of these celebrity urchins are completely talentless. No shock there, but there seems to be a lot of shock when it is exposed in the media or they snort something up their noses for the world to see – now this is a TV and *OK! Magazine* fact.

Swansea City are moving in to precious media circles, full of ignorance about the country we come from, the city our team represents and the history we have all been a part of – they will look elsewhere for their celebrity story. It goes without saying that a 'rich in stupidity' editor at a leading glossy magazine will look for glamour and column inches before putting in some graft to find the truth. This is all a part of the Premier League.

The celebrity 'where are they now' programmes in years to come will feature those characters that if most of us were asked about today, we would say 'who are they now?' Football is about celebrity to some, but to the real supporter it is not. And football, like most sports has a league ladder. This ladder stems from the lowly depths of amateur football which most of us have watched or played in, through semi-professional leagues, which I dabbled in (comedy value), through to a full-blown professional player, which I had not a chance in. It's your skills base and ability that earns you rewards in Association Football, not your plastic chest. So, we do have ground rules at least. Rules that we all abide by, even the most controversial or violent person can see the sense in this. My point is quite clear though, I do get, like you maybe, the odd person who says 'I can't see any sense in football, it's all a waste of time, kicking a ball about.' Well, that's good – at least they know what they like. I also know people who have said this, and who then have attended a few football games and are now ardent 100 per cent football fans. So it's a bit of a mix. You can get fame by shouting 'penis' on TV or for looking good while dancing like a monkey to someone else's song. Or you can also achieve fame through many hours of devoted practice, enhancing your ability and achieving the highest level you can in your chosen profession. Now, I am sure which one most of us would want to be – well, to an extent – and this is the difference between achievers and under-achievers, and indeed attention-seekers. In football the rewards are huge for being a success, even for attaining brief success – which unlike those who enjoy only fleeting, ephemeral fame because of their underlying lack of talent – that success is recognised for many years to come. Most people of a sporting bent remember the 1974 FA Cup final between Liverpool and Newcastle as an example, and if they don't they may well know who played, who scored and who won. But I don't think some halfwit in the *Opportunity Knocks* final of 1974 will still be remembered forty years later, will they? God bless them all the same. They tried hard, they just, for me, didn't try hard enough and the fact that none of us remember them proves that case.

The success for a city or country's football team changes attitudes, harmonises people and produces smiley faces – and an increase in beer sales and much happiness all round. A great thing for us all to be a part of, especially when it's sunny. That makes it even better. The outlook is good, in fact damned rosy; everyone is a part of something that is considered an achievement. This, I am afraid, doesn't happen after the *Britain's Got Talent, I'm a Celebrity, Get Me Out of Here!, Big Brother* or *Dancing on Ice* finals. And while that is the case I will remain of this opinion. This point is further proven by the open-topped bus around Swansea event as the club celebrated its remarkable achievement of reaching the highest league in the football ladder with the rest of the city. And of course the thousands and thousands who gawped, shouted and soiled themselves openly as the early evening procession crawled around Swansea after the Wembley play-off success. Everyone wanted to be a part of it, and as I mentioned in my previous book, that was a huge difference to what was going on nine years before when the support of the local council, mayor and all their hangers-on was needed the most. But that is the way life is, no one wants to know a loser, and the winner takes it all. However, victory is sweetest when you've known defeat.

That sweetness, for people like Leigh Dineen, Huw Jenkins and the many other board members, staff and players was evident on their faces as the invited staff attended the Lord Mayor's reception in the heart of Swansea with thousands rejoicing outside. I actually saw a few faces in that crowd probably as worthy as those invited to attend, but you couldn't squeeze everyone in, and anyway, we do need a refined structure, do we not? Or we would all be on the bus, and I have to say it looked pretty jam-packed to me as it was – a few of the, let's say, *weightier* Swansea board members looked in quite a precarious position going around those long and twisty tarmac corners. It was, though, a wonderful conclusion to a wonderful eight years of football success, so very fitting that Wales' number one football team would achieve that success after being away from the top flight for some twenty-eight years.

Those years were packed with so much frustration, jubilation and consternation that it would take a writer far more adept in the art form than me to catalogue it all. It was to be the start of a huge learning process for everyone. For fans it would be the excitement of travelling to places only seen on *Match of the Day*, and that list is celebrated throughout the football world. For the club it would mean getting a new fax machine and an instruction manual that actually made sense (I jest) and for the world's media it would be a chance to write some of the most idiotic football sentiment I have read for years (I do not jest). Indeed in certain cases some of the best football writing I have read on any Welsh club in a lifetime. For that alone it was worth waiting for. Now everyone wants to know us, and everyone wants to congratulate us for being Swansea City supporters. Friends who support other clubs would congratulate me as if it was I who scored a Wembley hat-trick, or it was I who lashed in the winner against Cardiff City next to dark, dark Ninian Park Road. However, I understood their sentiments, and in a way they were showing me how happy they were for me, how deeply understanding they were for my team achieving my new feel-good factor. It was a splendid summer of hope. The millions spent, well, nearly £10 million was fantastic, and gave the manager an opportunity to hope. We all knew that this brave Swansea City side would be no Derby County, and we all knew as well that we could turn a few established football sides over on the way. It would all come down to a few football firsts – the media would love those. The first home win, the first away win . . . the first this, and the first that. It would be open season on football firsts in Swansea, even appearing on *Football First* would be a football first.

The one-man team of Scotty Sinclair (or Frank or Trevor) plus ten would feature in all the best magazines and newspapers, as would the one-man team of many others plus ten before the season was out. Swansea WAGs would be interviewed (why, I have no idea – I don't care about any of them) and in one case invented links would be made that even the players were unaware of, and the football story would be written. The fixtures would be examined time and time again and pubs, clubs and new supporters would be planning their way across the country in their thousands. The club itself would need to find a way of making sure the benefactors of these away trips were the right ones – well, at least try to. The points, the prizes, the games, the days away, and all those nights would be filled with sentiment, hope and in a few cases tears. The songs will be sung, the drum will be banged and a ginger bloke will be banned for daring to have a loud percussion instrument about his person. It's all in folklore now. And it's all ready to be greeted by you in this book.

We did do battle, of course we did, we are Swansea, and we did our club and country proud. Welcomed by only a few, that Jack Army of 2011/12 was revered. And of course in the blue half (or more like a third) of Wales that green-eyed monster would return. Those pathetic statements to make themselves feel better about Swansea's failure in the Premier League would come back and haunt them time and time again. And when that was proven the second season syndrome no doubt will kick in. When *better* is a word only used in Swansea. *Better* team, league, players and fans. It's simple but so, so hard to understand when you have been brainwashed and abused (and done nothing about it) for so long. Our songs are now about our local rivals in the Premier League: West Brom, the Villa and Wolves and the established clubs in London, not Brentford and Orient (sorry, but its true), but Chelsea, Arsenal and Tottenham.

When we talk about visits to cup winners it is no longer in some paint trophy or Welsh Cup but we are visiting Champions League winners, finalists and contenders. And if I stop for a while, just a short while and think, then yes, we are in that league as well. We are to compete in a league that offers to us the Champions League. My word, we have arrived. No blue third will surely argue now, they must only aspire to be us. The ugly duckling has indeed turned into a swan. It shines and shimmers, it proudly flies and looks downwards on all that is below. You can't make a proud swan in flight out of Lego, but you can make a stadium out of it, and hope.

An old friend from Pembrokeshire rang me and said, 'I'm the happiest bastard there is, Keith,' and he was right – he is a bastard and he is a friend – and he sounded happy. He remembered that trip to Preston in 1981 that took two days to get home from. The car was abandoned on the side of the M6 and Ian Callaghan gave us a lift to the game. The hand-to-hand dabbling afterwards when all we wanted was a friendly taxi to the services (all in another book) and the explanations to our families on the Monday morning as to why it had taken two days to get home. He remembered those friends who followed and lost their own battles, be that to wives who no longer let them go to games, or to life itself, the real end game that no one wants to lose. To the players who have now long gone, to Robbie and all, we both smiled and laughed, and we paused for breath. To Ivor. To our Swansea City, our proud, oh-so-bloody-proud little football team in West Wales. A white ray of hope in so many lives – lives that are battered daily and torn apart. Communities that are ravaged and in despair have raised glasses to that football club, and the club has raised a fist in return. No fucking Saturday night talent programme matches that passion.

No words can describe this game of football to any man, woman or child who wants to know. You see, you have to go to know, and then if you do go, it may well get you and consume you. And whatever you are or want to be, or whoever you are or aspire to become, it levels us all. Every person is welcome you see, football in Swansea offers its hand. It is the hand that says you are welcome. Come and support us if you wish, or watch and support from afar. It matters not. No credentials are needed. To support this club it takes no money at all. You don't have to be the season ticket-holder or dutiful away supporter to be a Swansea Jack. You can just support and belong, be warm, be happy, belong. And when victory is with us you can feel that glow that all of us have felt, on many occasions we have loved and hugged and cherished every moment, every fatal pass or glorious move. The journey has twists and turns and real life burns, like this game, this football, this hope. It's life, it matters and it hurts like hell.

It is now time for our journey to begin, the season of Premier League. A season of firsts, then seconds and thirds. The season of hope and the season of belief. The season of us. Let's go comrades, and let's see what happens. Tell your families and friends you are busy, you are otherwise engaged for a week or two this year and next. The Jack Army is clearing its throats, the clinking of beer cans is heard, the excitement of new things is ahead, the next train departing this land is the last train of hope, and it's full of Swansea Jack Bastards.

It's time.

Chapter One

The Only Human in the League

30 May 2011

It's ten o' clock at night and I am pissed. The heat from the day and the stress washes away as I gaze upwards to the Gloucester skyline. I am holding a bottle of London Pride – I have been to London, so therefore it seemed a good idea. The date many of you will know, and many of you will remember forever. It's Monday 30 May 2011. You may be a new or even an old supporter, I don't really care. The sight of over 40,000 Swansea City supporters at Wembley, witnessing one dream at one time all sharing that one desire, will stay with me for the rest of my days. Be those days short or long, months, years or whatever, this day will be with me for every single second.

My head has been stained since 1968 with wanton and frivolous Swansea Town (then City) desires. I was indeed one of John Toshack's Black and White Army, and as many of you now know I was a long-lost punk rocker, come skinhead, come casual. So I will remain perfectly casual as I revisit that Bank Holiday Monday when my team Swansea City first cruised, then squeezed their way into a Premier League nobody said we would reach. A league that people laughed at when it was mentioned that we would. Those people, who now, by a strange coincidence are quiet, withdrawn and not evident at any level.

It has been at least sixteen hours since my mate reorganised the décor of my house by letting the dog out into a torrential downpour and battlefield-like garden, and then letting her back in again to ruin the kitchen and all that it was, and how I remembered it the night before. It seemed to me we had been on a pilgrimage, or maybe the word crusade is better? A lifelong desire for ultimate success that was the morning had been accomplished by the evening, our Sabbath day was a Bank Holiday and the principal players were those 40,000-plus Swansea souls.

You can only laugh and celebrate so much, and as the bile rose and the curve of a projectile lob hammered in to the dark, I felt much better. It was even fitting that I had successfully guided the day's beer and food onto a well-worn lawn and now had the freedom to enjoy more. If indeed I felt I could. This final act of the day was an exorcism. All the shit and bollocks that we all have had to put up with from the bilious no-marks in the press and the foolish writers of 'everywhere' in local and national newspapers had been truly splattered in vomit over a Gloucester landscape. Where are you now you 'true professionals' of the press in both England and Wales? Where are you now? I know you're sicker than I ever could be. Deep down you are hating this moment – your real team is beneath us, a downtrodden piece of mismanaged garbage beneath my feet. And in my current state I reckon that's exactly where you deserve to be. I have heard for years how this is your time, and this is the right team to achieve success for Wales and even from that ridiculous head-slapping man of years gone by I have heard how this team will represent the whole of the Principality. Oh really? What a joke. What a joker, and all who drove him and paraded with him, be they in prison, in court, in the newspaper or in the nude, I celebrate your lowly lives tonight. I am not bitter but I reckon I could fight them all this evening. One on one.

And then I collapse.

It must have been an hour later that I recall steadily and calmly pursuing a route through darkness in the garden to my greenhouse. Staggering slowly through a dense, dark night I find some form of solace in the thought that sleep will come far quicker in this space intended for vegetables and fruit. Yes, one more vegetable is coming to join you. I stagger one way, then the other, I find the wall of the house and then the line of the fence . . . this is incredibly time-consuming and I recall thinking 'this is taking far too long', then a large pole wedged itself in my crotch, knocking me down like a tenpin. This is really not the best way to end the day. Sitting there in the calm summer's night I gather what thoughts I can and try to recall the evening and the day. We got back from London at about nine o' clock, so I must have drunk quite a bit in the time between then and now. But of course I recall collapsing and falling around like the drunken man I was. I had only been drinking for half an hour tops, and then only a bottle of ale. That's very odd, one bottle can't do this to you – can it? The darkness swamped me again, knocking me down, penetrating my head and causing me to fall sideways to get more comfortable and to stop the nausea. This has not happened to me before that's for sure.

This is remarkably silly, very odd and all a part of the promotion process I thought. Four weeks later I would put two and two together (with the help of my GP) and realise that this was the first of my adventures in to the world of being diabetic. Drink had nothing to do with it . . . I was simply celebrating my new friend diabetes and Premier League football in one go. (From here on in we call him Dai.) On a day that was life-changing for Swansea City and all who work and play for the name, mine had changed as well. And equally as memorable as this may be for them, I reckon my life-changing event was unlikely to be rewarded with a £20,000 a week salary for playing in a white football shirt.

Bloody hell. What a pickle.

So that's the state of play, readers. However, the real state of play is a simple one. Swansea City have reached the Premier League when all around us, and close to us, have failed. The manner of the promotion, for me as a fan of some years now, has been in a way expected. I expected improvement as a club from the first day the board, as it was in 2002 and is today, took over the groaning old lady of the Vetch Field. In fact a truer statement would be that I should not in any way have expected improvement at all – the fact we had a club was a bonus. I think as football fans we expect a constant improvement in the state of harmony on and off the field at our clubs, and to an extent as a customer I suppose that is right. Of course you have to take into account the very fact that if it were not for the hard-fought battles of yesteryear, the fans' protests and all, more than adequately now covered, we *wouldn't* have a club at all. Question is, would you, me, us as fans of Swansea City now be over it if indeed we had succumbed to the great god of football failure, and been consigned to non-league football forever? Or maybe a worse fate – the end of the road as a club, full stop? Who would have thought it, Swansea City in the Premier League. So much to look forward to, and so much to hope for. After the past nine years of absolute and total football success.

In my last book, *Swansea City 2010/11: Walking on Sunshine*, I got the bit between my teeth from the very off as if exorcising another ghost – that is of the previous leaderships of the club. On this occasion unless I repeat it all again, there is no ghost to exorcise or blackguards to chase out of town. It's all a bit fine and dandy. Swansea City is shining, the world is lovely, and I have to change my diet. Excellent.

Of course straight away I am told by the experts who populate my life at work and in my various social circles that we will come straight back down . . . well that just goes to show how much they don't know. They wonder why their lives are so full of negativity, when all they can talk about is negatives. Someone, somewhere loves them – maybe. In a negative way no doubt.

Chapter Two

Here Comes the Summer

My main gripe in the 2010/11 season was the lack of recognition for the excellent football and management the club maintained throughout the hardest season it had encountered for a few generations. The eloquent way the manager put his views across, backed up by Colin Pascoe and Alan Curtis, two stalwarts of the club, and its achievements over a magnificent season was truly remarkable. Many will say that it's best to stay under the radar, but if the successes of this club are to continue, how long will that have to be the case? Immediately I am infuriated by the media; their lack of knowledge about the players, the stadium, the club, the team ethos, style of play and stewardship is alarming, almost shocking. Some idiot on TalkSport (there are many) sparks up and asks 'who is the Swansea money man?' Straight away I am incensed and have the desire to deliver a full-length Doctor Marten to his head via my telephone, but of course this is the TalkSport way. Make a silly remark, and get the callers lined up at 50p a minute, No, I will not make that mistake today, nor any other day. I feel there will be more of this as the season progresses; journalists with only an eye for the top six in the league having to trail down to West Wales, trying to fool the educated that they know about our club and its origins. They won't fool me, and I doubt they will fool you either.

Magnificence comes in many forms. In a footballing context it comes from well-placed free kicks – Fabio Borini springs to mind, or Mark Gowers' strike in the same game against Norwich last season. My mate Stokesy reckons it's a gleaming sea bass on the end of a big hook, a silvery, shining salty capture, ready for the pan in seconds, fried up with fennel and pepper with a squeeze of lemon.

Some people walk in to a room and light it up; they shine and create
a feeling of worth and success. Surprisingly Vinnie Jones has this
ability. Catherine Zeta Jones as well (my word I can hear you say
– this chap holds good counsel). For me the most impressive force I
have ever encountered in a brightly lit room is Robbie James, a man
who was as dominant off the field as he was on it, a true Swansea
legend. Today, looking at the Swansea squad I ask myself the same
question, where is the next Robbie James, if indeed that is possible?
The next Alan Curtis or John Toshack – do we have such ability
in this squad? In football terms I am sure we do, but in statesman
terms, in true and real Swansea terms, is there a character who is
able to make the walk from magnificence on the field to inspiration
off it?

Today as we move in to June I get the feeling that Fabio Borini
was happy to get the Swans to Wembley and into the Premier
League, but he had already done his deals and done his accounting
to manoeuvre himself back to his homeland, and Parma. Fabio may
well be a great international star of the future, he may well even
make that step to greatness, but it won't be at Swansea City. And
he states today he has no regrets, and neither have I. If the young
man that inspired the team to the Premier League sees his future
elsewhere, there is no loyalty from me, as there is no loyalty from
him. I wish him well, but feel the next time he bites his hand, for
whatever reason he bites it, he may well feel he has cut his nose off
as well. Darren Pratley will be moving on as well, he did so well in
the latter stages of last season, but knows deep down that he was
a bit-part player, never getting the appearances he desired. For me,
he was well managed by Brendan Rodgers. Every time Pratley got
an extended run in the team he tailed off in his enthusiasm as a
player, became stale quickly and only performed when he was being
challenged and in fear of losing his place in the side completely.
His goal against Forest apart, this side got to where they are now
without him in large chunks. He knows this and his pending move
to Bolton may serve him well. But Bolton? Where is the ambition in
that move?

I am hearing as well that Dorus De Vries wants some certainty
about his future which Brendan cannot offer, and rightly so. He has
been first choice for quite a while, but now we are Premier League
can we really offer a player the right to a jersey in the Swansea

team? He has deficiencies, does Dorus, and they are evident to us all; albeit a great goalkeeper he too will be moving on and Wolves have an eye on him. With that all going on as the transfer rumours and facts are made known, I get a call regards the future of Neil Taylor at Swansea City. 'He is having his head turned, Keith. It's looking like the vultures are circling, mate.' A player like Neil Taylor is a valuable commodity, discovered by Wrexham, but only after falling down elsewhere he is now a real asset to the club. His agent knows this too. Neil would have gone from £500 a week to eight times that at Swansea in one day, and now he is a Premier League player. Last season at Wrexham as he trained the summer away, he could never have dreamed he would be where he is today. Small steps, Neil, and thoughtful ones as well are needed. The Swansea faithful won't take kindly to a want-away defender, unproven and untested at the highest level. However, maybe like Darren Pratley he relishes a reserve team place elsewhere in the Premier League? Neil has had a superb season – he oozes quality, so it's difficult to understand his desire to move so quickly from the club that has given him so much.

Then there are the casualties – Cedric van der Gun, Albert Serran, James Grimes and Kerry Morgan are on their way. The best opportunity was van der Gun's; for reasons only known to him he didn't take it – he had the talent, but just let it slip through his fingers. The rest sadly are much clearer cases. I saw some glimpses of excellence in Morgan, but as a Premier League team I see the value in releasing all of them today. They still have their youth, and they still have their talent; it's not over yet for any of them by any measure. The only player who surprises many is Tommy Butler, a squad player who for me has shown only small doses of quality, and usually against Sheffield United! It seems, though, that Butler will be offered a new deal, and thinking about this logically, we do need a strong reserve side, hence Andrea Orlandi featuring in my thoughts today as well as Ashley Richards (Jazz) and the bright young talents pushing their way forward from the youth set-up. It seems we will be playing our reserve games at Llanelli, which is a sound move for Swansea City. It keeps the Liberty pitch in decent order before the rugby boys start chasing that big peanut about the place later on in the year, and is a decent setting for Premier League reserve team football.

I am pleased too that Danny Graham has signed, though the relentless moaning from Neil Warnock continues as he genuinely believes he should be a QPR player. What right he has to say this is beyond me, because if he should be a QPR player, he would be. Just because you invite someone round to your house doesn't mean you own them. What a guy that Warnock is. His constant harping on about his future will unsettle the club's owners, and may well force their hand.

Like many footy fans I love the summer break – endless days watching cricket scores on Sky TV, old men playing bowls down at my local club green, incredible really. I start to develop a fascination in the announcement of the first pre-season friendlies on Ceefax or an obscure desire to watch Welsh Football League teams in European competition. I think you may well be getting my drift here. For football reasons, the summer is pants. So – in more real terms the summer, albeit warm and delightful at times, is fucking boring. And added to this, the fact we are waiting for the Premier League fixtures to come out is equally frustrating. Swansea City news becomes a trail of lies and rumour from websites and equally frustrated journalists who are clearly about as wise to the Swansea City cause as they are to the state of Peruvian lower league football. They are clueless as to the Swansea football way, and even more clueless as to who in fact plays for us. Scott Dobbie is a player that seems to feature greatly in the newspapers of these so-called professional people, while another is the truly scintillating Trevor Sinclair, who also surfaces under the name of Frank. Bruce Dyer is another, when he is not being called Phil, that is. Recently I have been monitoring the progress of Liam Britton and Jeff Allen. These are just a few examples of lazy and uneducated journalistic attempts to understand the team that has travelled from the dark side to the Premier League.

The dark side for the London-based journalist will be *any team* bar maybe QPR, not in the south-east of England or any team outside of the Premier League, and even those in the Premier League will be served up only rarely at the end of *Match of the Day*. I am reliably advised by those who watch this programme that this will also be Swansea City's fate. We will slowly be relegated to the end of the programme and our season will end in the same way – with relegation. I suppose Swansea City v Bolton Wanderers is not going to set your imagination alight when you could be watching the greedy men of Manchester City play Liverpool, and their equally astute and old-fashioned manager Kenny Dalglish. Dalglish is a man so cemented in 1978 that he has prawn cocktail stains on his collar and traces of cheesecake on his chin. His nights in with the lovely Marina I am sure consist of glasses of Cinzano Bianco and snowballs followed by the ritual chomping of the contents of their fondue set. Football needs to move on, and £35m for Andy Carroll tells me all I need to know about Dalglish's prowess in the transfer market.

Fans are now beginning to wake up and see the new season ahead. Arsenal fans are still talking about signing £20m strikers, Manchester City fans believe a further £100m will secure the Premier League title, while fans of Darlington are collecting coins in buckets to save their club.

Football has such a divide, such a huge gap between the clubs in the pyramid system that the fans of the bigger clubs (easy to be one) talk in such massive figures they can have no concept of what £20m is or what it could really be used for. Any football supporter who follows a team starting in 'AFC' will know more about true fandom and passion than any gangsta outside the Emirates on a Wednesday morning doing their best to look exactly like the players they idolise. These are well-paid football players, indeed people who they regard as heroes, who will never recognise them nor care about them. That's a fact.

The plight of Darlington and Kettering Town concern me, because we at Swansea had the same fight as the fans of these clubs. The collections and the fight to rid our club of its cancer for five years was a long one. It was painful and pretty reckless at times, but our club came first. Those who lied their way in to positions of power were quickly met with an iron fist of hatred and a form of direct action that drove them all away back to the hovels and pits from whence they came. And I count a number of people in that statement, not just the obvious Pettys and Lewises of the time.

These days football clubs do come and go: Aldershot, Merthyr, Newport, Wimbledon and Halifax Town are obvious examples. Wimbledon are a favourite of mine, not a barnacle-type club like Queens Park Rangers. I'll talk more about that lot later (in football terms you understand, not as a generic exposure of hatred). By Wimbledon I mean the real Wimbledon, not the franchised stain that hangs around Milton Keynes like a poisonous cloud of despair. The fight AFC Wimbledon had, and FC Halifax to an extent, is the real football story and many should go and see what they did, like the Swansea City freedom-fighters of yesteryear. There are many others as well: Darlington first time around, Bournemouth, Doncaster back in the 1990s, etc. These football stories tell us more about our game than a thin and pasty-faced Arsenal fan sitting on those huge Emirates steps hoping for a glance of van Persie's well-fed face. I would rather spend time with Jimmy Pursey than be this awful type of football supporter, and that would have to be forced on me.

It is mid-June and I am so frustrated that I am reflecting a lot on the poor relations we have left behind, apart from the obvious green-eyed monster lurking down the road (not a sleeping giant), and I don't want us as a club or fans to end up like Arsenal's legions of empty-heads or Manchester United's national team, as big in Taunton as it is in Salford. In years to come I want Swansea City fans to know and realise what the club was and where it came from. The fight that was the early part of the millennium that led to a civil war to save the club must be remembered as much as any player. In fact far more.

Statues are not required. Fulham have Michael Jackson outside their ground, but what purpose does this serve? What is going on in the mind of their owner? Is there a business plan or model that requires this type of nonsense to be placed outside a club's ground; a club with a rich history and much tradition? Does it need a Jackson tribute? What have Fulham forgotten? Johnny Haynes? Eddie Lowe? Gordon Davies? Not a song, like Michael, of any purpose in any of them, but players (if players do shape clubs) who must be far further forward in the pecking order of public acknowledgement than Michael Jackson. My mixed point is this: we need to preserve what we have at Swansea, we don't need our history to be obscured by such people as Fulham have at the helm. Disastrous football management at board level needs focussing in on quickly when it appears, and it's the fans who need to ensure it is tackled. Better you fight the cause of your local club than enjoy the glory of a team like Manchester United from 300 miles away. Our 20 per cent interest at Swansea is so valuable.

Stone the crows, Leslie Harvey would be turning in his grave today. It's half way through June and the fixtures are out. And they have been really kind to us. First game away at Manchester City, then the next away game is Arsenal, then Chelsea. That's a guaranteed flyer for the Super Swans! The home games look far easier on paper, and that's where the similarity to anything the Championship threw at us ends. And let us not forget it's only three months ago that we lost at Preston, Burnley, Derby and Scunthorpe in a matter of six weeks. How anyone can say that we have guaranteed home bankers against Sunderland, Wigan, Stoke and West Brom is beyond me, but of course, I have been wrong before.

Now as I write this piece the boss is up Kilimanjaro with a few football buddies, and the cause is a heartfelt and poignant one for Brendan Rodgers. One of those buddies is the leftfield (without knowing he is) Chris Kamara, a man who once proclaimed to have discovered Jason Scotland in his second season at Swansea City. An incredible Lionel Richie lookalike with a personal quest to look daft whenever he can on the television, he seems to enjoy this role. A likeable misfit cast in the role of jester for his Sky TV compatriots to laugh at maybe, but when you have the prowess of Chris to discover players like Jason Scotland after they have scored 30 odd goals on TV, well, who am I to argue (insert smiley here)? And I have to say this – it isn't for me in this book to try to establish what feelings and emotions Brendan Rodgers is going through with family members affected by illness and personal tragedy. The recent loss of his mother and his father in the latter stages of cancer must be absolutely heartbreaking for such a young man. Suffice to say the way he continues to conduct himself and indeed take on this massive challenge says a lot about this man's character and personality. I really wish him well and a safe journey on yet another huge challenge in a year that has seen so many for our brave manager.

Talking of brave people, I really admired Bob Latchford when he played for Swansea City during our last visit to the top flight; a keen-as-mustard striker who had heaps of ability and a prowess in front of goal, in my opinion only matched by Gary Lineker in recent times. A superb striker and header of the old heavy football, before he left us for NAC Breda he was on the brink of an England call-up, and no Swans player has come close since. Bob tips us for glory in the Premier League, and believes genuinely that the side can hold its own in the top league in the world. I tend to agree now I read his thoughts. He, after all, knows his onions – he filled a few bags in his time – and his sentiments make me feel much better today. It's only a matter of weeks since our Wembley triumph, and I am getting all agitated with thoughts of failure and the club, my club, being a laughing stock. How daft.

Friendlies are being arranged, and a fairly highly priced ticket for the games against Real Betis and Glasgow Celtic (have they removed the Glasgow?) are announced, a joint ticket being purchased for both games saves a few quid. Oh well, in for a penny, lose a load of pounds. It's Premier League time, and we do need to make a smart start to the season. Even if it is a couple of friendlies. The games are a way off yet though and there is plenty more for me to get concerned about.

As predicted, Dorus has moved on – see ya mate. He says on the Wolves website these prophetic and interesting words: 'Wolves are a club with all the fundamentals in place to grow and expectations are higher than at Swansea at this moment in time.' The carefully chosen words of a man not wishing to upset the Swansea support, no doubt, but I do read between the lines a lot, as many of you do as well. This is rubbish from Dorus. If indeed he actually said it at all, and it wasn't his agent. He knows nothing of our club and its aspirations, he came too late to know and clearly took no interest at all while at Swansea to find out. I'm sticking with the competitive angle of his departure – that he is a keeper knowing that he could well be on the bench this season at Swansea City, and getting a salary in keeping with our keen and fairly administered wage structure. At Wolves he can earn more as a substitute warming the bench, and this I think may well be his philosophy. Do you blame him? He owes us nothing, and he was never a Roger Freestone, a player who turned down countless and far more lucrative moves away from Swansea season after season. I just can't see him making an impact at Wolves, and I can't see Wolves making an impact this season at all.

Grzegorz Sandomierski, a Polish Under-21 international, is being linked with us straight away. He seems an OK replacement, but I am also hearing we are after Michel Vorm of Den Bosch (always reminds me of a power tool) and now of Utrecht, though he will cost, I am told, up to £2m. There are a few other names I am not too familiar with. As much as the Swansea support are shouting for obvious (and very expensive) replacements for Dorus, I am keen to gen up some more on Vorm. He sounds a Brendan-type acquisition, no doubt via our ever-increasing Dutch network of contacts very ably assisted I am sure by a certain keen and enthusiastic Swansea City director. And for this reason for me, he is a favourite to sign. Sandomierski could be a good back-up keeper to a real number one, and as I get contact from certain quarters in the know on these matters, it really does confirm to me that Dorus could have and indeed, probably would have been a replacement this season. It all becomes clearer.

Then more madness. Marcos Senna is keen to sign for us, this is incredible, he's not a bad player, but is he right for us? Spanish player of the year a few seasons back, he's too old I think and it strikes me he will want a big wage to cement his friendship with Santander. These are the players we have to be mindful of, the players with one eye on the big pot of money they perceive the Premier League has, and now at Swansea. The players with no reason to be in any way loyal to a club they didn't even know existed two seasons ago. Players looking for one more big payday.

I am more interested in the signing of Stephen Caulker from Tottenham on loan, a real Brendan Rodgers signing, a player being referred to as 'the future' (like garlic bread?) and one who Harry Redknapp believes will flourish in the Swansea City pure football domain. Currently an England Under-21 international and born in Feltham, London, I am hopeful he will settle as well as Leon Britton did when he ventured west all those years ago. He looks a real prospect, and talking of prospects, I don't think he will sign for us no matter what kind of season he has. Harry definitely wants him at Spurs next season if all goes well. Caulker hasn't played for Spurs at all, he only has what could be described as a promising youth career, so I am not sure if he will be ousting Garry Monk any time soon, but of course Garry does carry the odd injury. So, can Stephen Caulker step in to his shoes? I think this is what enthuses Brendan as a manager – getting a hold of a young player and nurturing the talent he sees in his ability. This must be the pay-off for any manager like Brendan, someone who studies the game, and collates information on styles and types of coaching which he turns in to a specific training ethos, which he has done so well at Swansea City.

He has the ability, as well, to converse in a number of languages and to display a level of intelligence above the average Premier League manager. Indeed there are any number of merry-go-round money merchants who see football as a sweet shop for their own greed, and who are regularly seen stealing the proceeds of a club's wealth with no remorse, which makes Rogers' style all the more refreshing. See how I go off on one now and again folks? Thing is, with Brendan you don't see him getting into verbal fights with other managers, representing our club professionally without Pardew-esque bawling and shouting in other people's faces, or Wenger-style tirades like a spoilt boy. Brendan does seem to be the absolute professional incarnate. Remarkable.

The media refer to him as the failed manager of Reading, or the man who left Watford for better things. However, today, on this very warm and breezy end of June day, Brendan is a Premier League manager, a man who has laid more ghosts to rest this season than any manager I can think of. The Premier League bus parade is history, the clamouring well-wishers from Swansea's councillors to the mayor (so noticeably absent when the club needed help) have gone, full of wine and song, as cheery as they can be and all to a man and woman confirmed Swansea City supporters. These people are purely historical pictures in the *South Wales Evening Post*. For the annals of history they reflect nothing more than joy, painted pictures of the moment – no anger, no frustration, just enjoying the ride, on the back of the work of the few, now they want a piece of the glory. They laud the team and its players, slapping the backs of the fans who now run the club, who mercilessly worked to secure a bright future, when a ticker-tape parade was far from their thoughts. The evenings of misery as private lives in some cases, were torn apart to provide the city with a team to be proud of, not a peanut-chasing team, but a real football team. A team of heroes, some say 'bit-part players', but they say it without knowing the true story.

Laughable in the extreme is my current pet hate, Ipswich Town. Their chief executive, Simon Clegg (never trust a man called Clegg, they don't know what side they are on) sniffing a few quid out via the Tamás Priskin loan from last season has asked the Premier League to place an embargo on Swansea City. This is over owed money due to Priskin's return to Portman Road prematurely through injury. Huw Jenkins responds, and thankfully stands his ground on this matter. Quite professionally, and clearly learning new media skills at an alarming rate, our Huw looks sternly in to the camera and states in his best diplomatic voice, 'I'll be in touch.' This may well conjure up thoughts of horses' heads and lonely locker areas in deserted train stations as Huw, dressed in black, manoeuvres his way quietly in search of his quarry, poison-tipped brolly at the ready, delicately poised to pounce with a getaway car parked outside. He is a football fan remember, we hold grudges. Ipswich no doubt will get their extra dosh, Swansea no doubt with millions banked can afford it. What's the problem? Only Clegg knows, and looking at the media's reaction and that of Jacks all over the world, only Clegg cares.

The way that football spins its plates is difficult to predict, which is why I suppose we all love the game. The unpredictability from one week to the next, and the unpredictability as well of the fans and the game itself draws us all to the places we worship. I support Swansea City because in the late 1960s I was taken to the place we now know as 'The Old Lady', the Vetch Field, Swansea. I don't worship the players, as many of you know from previous ramblings, I enjoy my club and what it achieves. I like the unsung hero to get the plaudits, the fans who care and matter, not the £20k a week Premier League player. And now this season I am sure we will have a few of them. The player that all of a sudden wants a taste of the champagne reception, the lovely stuffed Premier League banquets of five-star food and the gorgeously prepared bank statements. That's the player – no longer dripping in Swansea blood, but Premier League gold. The ceiling for our spending will no doubt increase to this maximum amount. However, I cannot be a supporter who calls another man a 'god' and has this status plastered on my back. For me, it's all a bit strange to sing another man's name and claim I am indeed, in love with him. Not that this is in any way a statement as to my sexuality, it purely does not float my boat to sing a man's name, be they Brendan, Joe or Danny. Or indeed Roberto Martinez. If I proclaimed my love for Roberto back when he managed our team, I would be bitter when he left, remorseful of his lack of faith in my support for him. And like so many now would be so, so bitter and angry still, even though much water has travelled under the bridge since he went to Wigan. Players and managers will leave, we know this, and when they do certain players and managers inspire so much anger and aggression in the supporters for leaving. I don't think I want that emotion dictating my daily feelings for my club. It isn't healthy. Giving players a god-like status and other unconventional emotional outbursts of love for another human being are not, I am afraid, my reason for supporting Swansea City.

Have you got it?

Chapter Three

July 2011: Tinker Taylor

Well, well, well, Neil Taylor has signed a four-year deal at the Liberty. Whatever possessed him to kick up such a racket in the first place really did surprise me; as already documented, he was on £500 a week this time last year. Little steps Neil, little steps. You're a Premier League player now, and will no doubt get more starts than stops in this Swansea side, and that new deal really does increase the chances of financial stability for life eh? Get in there, let's enjoy what we have for a moment.

Neil Warnock is a manager that you either love or hate: he says he is like Marmite. I would say he is more like paint stripper – you keep it in the garage for a few months, and only when you need it for a one-dimensional task do you open the lid. He has tabled a bid for our Ash, £2m is the derisory amount on offer. Incredible really, and it's only when you see bids like that you realise why QPR found it so difficult to secure Danny Graham. I get a very excited phone call from a well-worn-out contact shouting about Eidur Gudjohnsen signing for us, he is so keen in fact it's all a done deal, but I do know differently. There will be a number of stalling points for the club, especially the value he puts on his wages compared to what we as a club think he is worth. I know that like many players he is seeking out one more lucrative contract, and I get the impression that Swansea City are not the sort of club to offer such things. This one will run for a bit more before smoothing itself out a bit. Even his old man Arnur is in on the act, talking up the prospects of his son joining either Swansea or West Ham; clearly it's a money move, because West Ham are a Championship club and Swansea are not. It's a no-brainer if you want to play top-flight football, so it has to be cash, and greed again that is winning the day. That is my humble opinion, nobody else's, and definitely not one whispered in a dark corridor.

My old mate Andrea Orlandi has signed up for a bit longer. He is a player who, as you know, I have reservations about. He has bags of ability, but in our hardworking midfield I struggle to see where he fits in. Àngel Rangel has also signed a contract. Then a writer called Sachmaster on the interestingly named 'football blog' website proudly predicts that Swansea are key certainties to be relegated from the Premier League. He bases this on the fact that teams struggle coming up from the Championship – well, no shit Sherlock – but he also displays his ignorance as to what is happening in West Wales by talking about one player – Scott Sinclair. Such ignorance in so many writers, be they amateurs like this person or the crowned gold media, will go in our favour as the season progresses, I am certain. The goalkeeper situation lingers on with Fulham's David Stockdale stating he would love to sign for the club, on loan that is. Like Dorus I think he believes we may well struggle. He is a cracking keeper, and if we do face any difficulties signing him it will come in the small print regarding his loan period. I reckon that we want a permanent keeper and not a loan keeper. So maybe that's going to be in big print. Stockdale on loan will not work for us at all.

What cracks me up is the way we do get associated with old players, and this time its Jason Scotland: no, no, no we don't need him back, he has already fallen flat on his face in the Premier League with Wigan! We don't need to reinforce his ability in front of goal, which will be lacking at the highest level, and this will be to our detriment. Jason is a cracking choice when you need an equaliser against Bristol Rovers with five minutes to go in League One, but I am not so sure if he is the answer in the same scenario at Old Trafford. Last season I know he may well have been a short-term solution, but the greed (here I go again) of the deal meant there was no way that Jason Scotland was going to sign for us. Remember our board? It just isn't going to happen Jase, and to be honest Ipswich Town haven't conducted themselves at all well with us over the past few months. Greed comes in many forms, adult communication could easily have made things happen, but when you have Paul Jewell at the helm, well, what do you expect? We are better off without Jason Scotland, and that is a fact.

July has started in earnest hasn't it? So day in and day out we are getting bombarded with has-beens, old players, new players and downright ridiculous signing suggestions. I bet Huw's top drawer is jam-packed with agents' DVDs of all the best bits of players who wouldn't even get a kick at Barnet let alone Swansea City. Marvellous stuff, but it is really getting to boiling point, and as someone with more than a vested interest in the FIFA licence and for licensed agents, I find the dealings, manipulation and media strangulation during these times literally fascinating.

Wayne Routledge is a realistic proposition, a player with bags of speed and ability who, if managed correctly, will slot nicely into the squad. The money on offer is approaching £1.5m, but I reckon it will take a few quid more to tempt Newcastle to deal with us. They are still smarting over the Neil Taylor ramblings (I hope they choke on it) and will be a difficult demon to keep tied down if they want to be difficult and fight. The way they went about the Neil Taylor business still leaves a nasty taste, I just wonder how they knew he had a buy-out clause? Well actually, I don't wonder, but I am sure you know what I mean. Of all the possibilities Routledge is the most nailed-on I reckon; he is just what we need. He needs to come to us focussed and ready to improve and manoeuvre himself in to the Swansea City way, but I find this type of player and talk of us involved in this type of player exciting.

Then Leicester get involved and the Milan Mandarić legacy comes snooping and sniffing round the hard work of others. Lazy opportunists looking to feed off the work that Swansea are doing to secure bright futures for the club. There are a lot of clubs like this – lazy to the core – too stupid to put the graft in to get a better day for their supporters. I read that Routledge is their player. The Newcastle fans' blogs report the signing first, then the *Daily Mail*, and the £1.5m we have had accepted is forgotten. It's the same scenario now as the Gudjohnsen deal, just which way will Wayne tip? Championship football or Premier League football? What drives him the most – money or pedigree? The *Mirror* now reckon it's a straight run in between QPR and Leicester, and it's at moments like these that I place faith in the Swansea board and the manager. They thrive on this, like I do, like we do. Now Nottingham Forest (Notts Forest) are in on the deal, sniffing around. It's a straight sprint now between money or glory for Wayne. I get the feeling Newcastle would love him to go anywhere but Swansea City.

We are half way through July, the Swans are playing cricket for charity in Mumbles and apparently Gudjohnsen is ready to snub

Swansea for West Ham. Go on then mate, but I will let you in to a secret, your wage demands meant you got snubbed a week ago. I wonder what his old man has to say now? Tonight Neil Taylor signed for Swansea proper after ironing out the longevity of the agreement, four years is a good deal all round. Trialists feature heavily at all clubs in and around this time and we are no different, German goalkeeper Thorsten Stuckmann and Brazilian midfielder Radamés Martins Rodrigues da Silva are running around in Swansea Bay, and like you I have never heard of either of them. Stuckmann is a second division German keeper (rated by some good contacts) and Silva as stated is Brazilian, but does that make him any good? Again I am told they are very much (very, very much) on the fringe of things and are not likely to get a contract offer. Swansea are looking for players who can be moulded into the 'Swansea way' and for that reason it doesn't only matter what you do on the pitch, it's how you fit in off it, and what you add as a personality to the dressing room.

I am reliably told that Tommy Butler has personality in abundance, which to some degree has earned him a further one-year deal at Swansea (or should I say stay of execution?). He will only feature in the reserves this season, that much is a nailed-on fact. However, this is rather good business, Tommy Butler, with Orlandi and a few other players from the Championship campaign like Luke Moore, Craig Beattie and Stephen Dobbie will add to a reserve side in a decent and competitive Premier League reserve system.

Now I am not mocking anyone in particular, but the reoffending of Swansea City when it comes to signing players from outside these isles is becoming legendary. And indeed David Edgar springs to mind, the Canadian player from Burnley. There is a lot of paperwork to complete when deals are struck, and two football associations to advise, but we do need to look at our practices regarding this. I am not one to knock the club too often, but professionalism in sport is no different to any other business, and we need to get this sorted out. Or maybe it's our processes that need sorting out. I know of clubs which, when they sign a player, they employ an agent or individual (they don't have to be licensed) to travel to the club the player is being signed from to ensure the administration is carried out appropriately. In fact I know of people who do this for a job, and it pays pretty well. Relying upon a club during a last-minute deadline day deal to get certain things right on your behalf is leaving things to chance. Now, I am not in any way saying we need to reinvent our processes for this, I am just saying we don't need players believing they have signed when they haven't. Or indeed being talked about because a player has not signed, when the process is really just par for the course. If it is a fact we need to resign from the FA of Wales (hallelujah! I hear you say), then so be it, if it's a case that paperwork is being stalled as a result of others, then hit them hard, and if it is an in-house issue, get them trained! We are now Premier League.

I only say this because a fairly decent prospect in Jonathan Parr is on our radar, and a number of other clubs are interested. Not in the Premier League as such, but he is a young raw talent. He plays for Ålesund in Norway, and speaking to a friend who knows about Norwegian players he reckons he may well be one for the future. However, Jonathan Parr does not see reality. His recent quotes about 'letting my agent sort things out, and when he has I will be interested' do not help him. Swansea City slowly lose interest, the agent playing the usual game of press speculation (sorry manipulation) and Jonathan Parr signs for Crystal Palace as a result. A missed opportunity for him more than Swansea City – he will quickly find this out. I hope the club is able and ready to secure players like Parr quickly when the need arises. We are looking at quite a few foreign-based players, so I am just slightly concerned that we have the right mentality to get this in order. The days of Robin Sharpe and the fax machine are long gone, and I am sure they will never return.

It doesn't surprise me that Sky Sports are to screen the Manchester City away game live next month when it all kicks off, and it doesn't surprise me too much that Ryan Bertrand of Chelsea will not be coming to Jackland on loan. I say this after Premier League Swansea City lose 1–0 at Neath, but it isn't all bad news. Once again thousands of Swans fans are there, and the side is really experimental. Stuckmann gets a game in goal and looks a bit shaky, his trial could be reaching an end, and looking at the side, I can't see too many if only three starting come Premier League kick-off weekend. Dyer gets a sprint out, as does Scott Sinclair, and that's about it. Oddly enough Swansea City are playing in three hours' time at Port Talbot as well, so a plethora of Swansea teams playing all over the shop is the order of the day.

This is all very Premier League. The Swans stuff Port Talbot 3–1. More experimentation and bluffery from the sidelines, Brendan choosing to shove in Craig Beattie, Lee Lucas, Ferrie Bodde, Alan Tate and Joe Allen. The Swans look more purposeful, and the scoreline could have been more. There is little intensity: it's July, it's hot, so little is learned, by the fans at least, but these are calm games before the Premier League storm. The sneaky signing of keeper José Moreira from Benfica has little to do on the pitch, and chats with the fans. David Cotterill has a few things to prove if he doesn't want to join Tommy and Andrea in the reserves, but doesn't do it for me, and over the two games in one afternoon maybe ten ex-Swans are on show as well for the opposition.

The fact that Brendan still wants more keeper cover and José Moose Moreira is now confirmed as a contact tells me he is still not happy with what he has got between the posts. Lee Camp is now a genuine contender, but I know Forest will want millions for him. Does Lee Camp want to expose himself to another Championship season at Nottingham Forest (Notts Forest)? The side looked so jaded after being outplayed by Swansea last season in the play-offs; I would say they could well implode, in true Cardiff style. Camp would be a great signing, but Michel Vorm is heading our way too, from Holland. This is put into even sharper focus as Yves Ma-Kalambay is not offered a new contract at the club, I can't imagine why. Must be that he isn't good enough?

Moving on quickly . . . we have David Cornell on the out on loan roundabout, Dorus has gone, so has Yves. All we have left is José Moreira. We probably need two keepers, and Brendan wants them before the summer warm-down (winter warm-up) camp in Austria. Here's hoping Brendan. There will be a £2.5m bid put in for David Stockdale; Fulham value him at so much more it all feels a bit half-hearted.

The keeper situation I am sure will resolve itself, and unlike Roberto's rationale for goalkeepers (we will get one in if we need one) at least we are trying to get it sorted and have a squad capable of doing something really sound this campaign. This for me was one of Roberto's real failings, getting loan keepers in when the one keeper we had was injured. He talked about a system, he went on about a philosophy, then got Artur Krysiak in on loan from Birmingham City's second reserve side, utter madness. And it cost us.

The thing I am really enjoying at the moment is the disorientation surrounding the introduction to what the club are calling 'Jack Army Membership', an idea based on rewards for attending games as the season progresses. Certain games give you a certain amount of points, the bigger games like Liverpool and Manchester United away will obviously have literally thousands of supporters wishing to go. To get a ticket you need to have acquired an amount of points (yet to be decided, or maybe yet to be revealed) to get a chance of getting a ticket for these very high-profile games. This scheme costs £10 for the season. I have signed up, but as a season ticket-holder it may well be a consideration that getting to all the home games is a bonus in itself. Of course, I need to turn the screw a bit as well to get to as many, if not all the away games I can. Luckily I have a few decent contacts, and a creative spirit to push forward this area of my football fandom. Not everyone has this. I'll enjoy that for now. The scheme will generate a fair few thousand pounds for the club that's for sure, but that's clearly not the reason for introducing it. There is a sense of fair play to the idea, which I like and will get those supporters to games they wouldn't have stood a chance of getting to, all for a £10 investment. Even those without season tickets get the same tier structure to purchase tickets for games, and this is set at £25. Don't knock it.

Then for the religious 500 or so, there is the away season ticket. For £900 you are guaranteed a ticket for all away games. At the end of the season the total amount laid out for each game is added up and the money left over returned to you. So for about £1,350 this season you can get an East Stand ticket for home games and a guaranteed away ticket as well. Many will take this up I am sure. I know of quite a few who have, and fair play to them for having thirty-eight weeks out of the season to get to every game. Let's not forget though the travelling and food, maybe the odd programme as well, and other supplementaries. I see the season panning out like this financially: with the £1,350 for home and away games and then an approximation of £50 a game for petrol, travelling, food, etc. – on top of that (I am being generous) some fans travel and stay over as well – the total for this inaugural Premier League campaign will be in the region of £3,400 to watch Swansea City play. I am sure there are many supporters not looking in to this as deeply as I just have, because if they did then they may think twice. Disposable income is nowhere near the levels it was a season or so ago, owing to our beloved government choosing when we are and when we are not 'in this together'. It is one hell of a commitment. Albeit that if like me, you are not bothered about missing the odd game, then the pressure comes off a bit. There was a time when following Swansea City was not that difficult to do, not only now do we have to look at the financial aspect, to be rewarded with seeing every game, you need a wealth of cash in your back pocket.

I also know many fans who travel together (husbands and wives, partners, etc). Now this is where your loyalty is tested, because for both of you to go to every game, and witness what will be an incredible season, you would be left little change out of £7,000. Are you reading this my dear overpaid Premier League player? That's nearly half a week's wages for you and that's at the lower end of the Premier League salary scale. Yes, because some Swansea City players will be on £14,000 a week, and in some cases a lot more. By the way, let's pause for a second: £14,000 a week is £56,000 a month, making a three-year contract worth £2,250,000. I wonder if that salary requires careful household management and direct debits to cover utility bills?

Never before has there been such a disparity between fan and player in West Glamorgan.

I will add to that. I believe that at some point throughout the season – maybe January, maybe before – a clever and astute commercial practice will be to announce 'early bird' season tickets for season 2012/13. This will also require financial consideration. Every club does it, and we will certainly be foolish to ignore this ticketing ploy. Many clubs announce these deals in December (around Christmas time) and offer deals ever-increasing up to the end of the season to renew the season ticket. The saving on average is £60. If Swansea City do this, and as I said they would be foolish if they don't, more money leaks from that back pocket of yours. This extra outlay of £450 or so for another season ticket will increase this year's expenditure to watch Swansea City for two people to £8,000 to watch and be guaranteed a ticket until May 2013. The club will definitely do this in my opinion, because if Swansea City get relegated the revenue will fall somewhat. So get the offers out while it's looking rosy, capture the audience at their weakest. You as a fan will hardly recover the extra season ticket money outlaid this season as long as the team are a success, because the same thing will happen season in, and season out. And remember the queues outside the Liberty when the last of the season tickets went on sale in June and July when Premier League fever was at its height in South Wales? Trust me, there will be a fair few thousand more just waiting for your moment of weakness who will snap up your ticket very quickly indeed. And then, no matter how much you earn, you won't get in.

This is the price we pay. In fact it's the price we all pay if you want to watch Swansea City this season, and next season. Many I know just cannot afford it, average salaries are not £14,000 a week – in some cases that's all there is for a whole year's work, and then there's tax to consider. And this isn't disposable income for one person, this is what you survive on, what you need in the bank to keep your life intact. In many cases, whole families depend on this income, so the figures above on an average £16,800 a year salary, even if there are two of you earning, just do not compute. Could you spend a third of your income before tax on Swansea City? Or more to the point would your other half, dependants or whatever, want you to jeopardise their basic needs to watch the club we all love? I know many of you earn more, and I also know many fans who don't earn at all. They say football is a drug, and by any reckoning this season, you will need to outlay the average amount a dependant drug user does in one year to get your football fix. Trouble is, there is no NHS prescription for those who can't afford it. Not even a free one in Wales.

My football life has gone full-circle so many times I don't often see the wood for the trees at times. Luckily I am not in a financial position of dependence on others, nor do my musical and footballing ventures stem the quality of life my family enjoy. I am one of the lucky ones, albeit a lucky one who has taken twenty-five years of hard graft to get where I am today. As a writer I don't earn fortunes, but it helps out with the costs that I have outlined here. I love the club, and even though I did say a season or two ago I would be happy to stay in the Championship, that maybe was tinged with the feeling that I never really thought we would get in to the Premier League. It was a safety net. An emotional fallback, because I felt that we were being tolerated all round by all teams, the Championship was as good as I thought it would get. And yes, there are times when

I think back to our long minibus (and coach) trips out of Gloucester to Hartlepool, Scunthorpe and Barnet, and wonder if they were the halcyon days and not these.

Getting Dave the weatherman's annual pie and ale book out and choosing a decent pub with great food, and then getting so full up on local ale we didn't care if we got to the game or not – that was our distant football past. There were so many times I felt like this at half-past two, generally on a Saturday afternoon, 10 miles from the ground we were meant to be at, that it became a warning of the game to come. We generally lost the game when this type of feeling swept over you, but now, I wouldn't miss this journey for the world. If I could be in the ground at eleven o'clock in the morning I would. That's this journey this year, our Premier League year. The journey many of us have been on over our supporting lives has been a lifetime of journeys, as I said, many full-circles. Many emotions. This season is so different. For those of you who managed to get the last book before it went off the scale (four times is the current reprint count) those new editions were quickly bound by my hardworking and tolerant publishers – you will know that the football camaraderie we all get from a group travelling together. This has always been foremost in my mind. I remember better those excruciating results away from home for the fact we travelled as one, and enjoyed the day – as one.

I am in no way complaining about footballers' wages, agents, clubs, directors, boards, grounds or fans. It's all a part of the package. I can opt in or I can opt out. I am merely pointing out the complexity of success for the football supporter. I decided to sign up for this and I can opt out whenever I like. As long as we stay in the Premier League, be that for one season or ten, I could never have written the script for the way it all unfolded. Which turns me to my original point: that's why we go to games of football, that's why we are supporters of Swansea City. It's the unpredictability of the day, the whole all-consuming majestic ride we get on as these exciting football days commence. You could never predict the outcome, I leave that to the football pundit, the same pundits who describe Leon Britton as a journeyman footballer. Like that statement, they often get it all wrong. As I look at the fixtures today I see Manchester City, Tottenham, Chelsea, Manchester United, Liverpool, Newcastle and Villa all ready to take on the mighty Jacks. Down the road they have the usual Championship fare, and for that reason alone I wouldn't change it for the world, not any world, especially the outdated one I hear about so often from East Wales.

Live for today and live for the future, not for 1927 or indeed 1981. I feel humbled, gracious and proud. And I think I can thank the players for that, among many other Swansea-related people – yes, even I can stretch to that. Loyalty does come in many forms, be that the one-game-a-season supporter who scrimps and saves to keep their family happy and healthy and takes their chance to see the Swans when they can, to the all-out home and away fan who wouldn't miss a game even on a Boxing Day when a taxi journey is all that is needed to get to Crewe. We come in many shapes and forms, and from a whole host of places.

So as stated, José Moreira has put pen to paper. There isn't too much known about the guy, but as a replacement for Dorus he stacks up . . . sort of. By that I mean he has been about for a while now, and is nearly thirty years of age, a man with quite a few years left by goalkeeping standards and who has featured for his country via Benfica at Under-17, -19 and -21 levels. It took him a while to make his mark as an international and so far he has one appearance from 2009, so maybe he is improving with age. I am hearing, though, that Brendan wants three goalkeepers, not including David Cornell who is already being considered for a loan move, just for the season. The goalkeeping situation is far from settled, and with the season not too far away and a few friendlies lined up we should be thinking more positively about getting the right number one in to the side. Michel Vorm crops up again; it's taking ages if we really are after him. Maybe Brendan is convinced he has his man, and it's just time that will dictate the Dutch international putting pen to paper. I am not so sure, I am hearing conflicting stories, it isn't as easy as it once was to get these things confirmed with lazy journalists churning out nonsense wherever and whenever they can with little concern over the accuracy or integrity of their stories. My confirmed and tested sources all state that Vorm is stalling, but is looking like he will sign.

We have had games at Neath, Port Talbot and Afan Lido as well as the upcoming friendlies against Celtic and Real Betis. I am hearing a game against an Olympic side from the UAE is in the planning stages. How very 2012! The game against Celtic comes on a Wednesday evening, which will be the first game since that mad, mad night against Nottingham Forest. Then it's Real Betis on a Saturday afternoon – nothing can go wrong in these games, win, lose or draw, it's just a case of getting back in to the football mindset for players and fans alike. Betis have already stuffed Havant & Waterlooville 7–0; no surprise there.

Garry Monk, Nathan Dyer and Joe Allen are all talking up their contract ambitions, and in Garry's case I see this as an ideal opportunity to reward the club captain with at least a year's work. I genuinely believe he can come in at times and hold the fort, he knows our ways, and knows our style. The other two are no-brainers. I simply love the Brendan Rodgers responses to the local Welsh league friendlies. Some newbies to the Swansea-supporting game are suggesting we should be playing bigger clubs. Absolute nonsense. Brendan states, and quite rightly so, that local league sides need to feel the rewards of what Swansea City are achieving as well. A simply fantastic answer to his critics regards the pre-season campaign and it is truthful as well. His transparency once again shines through. There must be at least ninety-one other Football League clubs extremely envious of the Swans. Afan Lido experienced a strong Swansea side on the weekend, a team of two halves this time with an easy 2–0 victory for us. The squad now go to Austria for further conditioning as we build up to the big two friendly games against Real Betis and Celtic. Post-match Brendan speaks of values and personalities, conditioning and belief . . . and all this after a 2–0 victory over Afan Lido? I am impressed.

The Austria trip is being called a training camp, some Swans fans who make the games call it a piss-up, others a holiday and one whom I know well, an adventure. At least Betty from Port Talbot won't be there . . . will he? Inter Baku will feature in one game against the Swans and then the UAE Olympic team. This isn't really a fans' trip, but a few get out there. It's no Palamós in the sun from two years earlier when thousands made the journey, and it's a tad cold as well. The venue will be a place called Obertraun outside Salzburg, and a desperate coach journey from Munich is the Swans players' treat, it can take up to six hours! Everton have been here before, as have Dunfermline and Chelsea reserves! I am reliably told in the quiet mist of an alpine evening that Paralimni, a team from Cyprus, also lurk close by doing what the Swans are doing, getting ready for the season ahead. I wonder if anyone else hasn't heard of them either?

It was a hard-fought journey – one that didn't require too many penalties to decide, but a lot of patience. Expired passports, excuses for late arrivals and lost luggage are all a part of the experience for the Swansea squad. Nothing goes smoothly when thirty-odd folk travel together on a plane and coach to Austria. Team bonding doesn't just happen in full sight of the cameras and press with a ball on a pitch – it comes in many shapes and forms. Danny Graham standing on a stool singing 'Mr Brightside' by The Killers is a highlight, or indeed not, depending on your point of view. He was followed by Caulker's corking rendition of 'Amarillo' by Tony Christie and a Black Eyed Peas effort from the new keeper José Moreira was rounded off by Ryan Harley's 'Sex on Fire'. I hope they play better than they can sing. The players are getting along brilliantly and the manager is beaming.

More good news as Daniel Alfei, Ashley Richards (Jazz), Lee Lucas and Joe Walsh are all included in the Wales squad to play Hungary at the County Ground, and home of my favourite non-league team Haverfordwest County, or the Bluebirds as they are known. Yes I know, very unfortunate, and the coming season sees my hometown club in the doldrums on and off the pitch. They have been relegated from the top flight of Welsh league football – no more S4C live games on a Saturday afternoon for the Bluebirds.

I don't like phone calls at eleven o'clock at night, but I do appreciate this one as it gives me time to think over the signing of Leroy Lita from Middlesbrough for a lot of money. More than I thought we would pay, if I am totally honest. With Danny Graham in the strikers' box seat, Craig Beattie and Luke Moore already at the club, Lita seems an odd signing from Brendan. He is only twenty-six, though it seems to me he has been around for many years and we pay nearly £2m for his services, so surely he is very much in the manager's plans? Leroy has had the odd incident during his career with the authorities, and to me he always looks like he is about to start rucking. He prowls around the pitch with that thrusting look about him. I like that. He is back in the Premier League as well, probably about where he deserves to be on ability. Tony Mowbray, his manager at Middlesbrough, baffles me though. It's not hard I know, but he says, 'Good luck to Leroy , he wants to play in the Premier League, so good luck to him. If he comes back I am sure he will battle hard to get back in the team.' What the hell is he on about? Clearly Mr Mowbray isn't aware that Swansea have actually signed him!

The Austrian experience was useful, and the squad in lovely new Adidas kit look the business as local keeper Gerhard Tremmel has a run out and looks very impressive indeed. I shouldn't do him a disservice; he once played for Bayern Munich and recently Salzburg – that's the local connection. Tremmel also played against Juventus and Manchester City last season in Europe, so he ain't no slouch. The German may well get a look-in if the keeper situation becomes serious and Moreira is the only other choice, and anyway I say sign him now, he used to play for the brilliantly named Energie Cottbus. The squad relax in the beautiful surroundings of Lake Halstatt and climb the impressive Dach Stein Welterbe, which is nothing compared to Brendan Rodgers' magnificent feat in Tanzania, but hits a few players quite hard. Nobody likes heights, but it seems that Ashley Williams doesn't like them at all.

The real test of the gathering apparently comes in the form of Inter Baku. I am not so sure; when you look at them as a side they are decent for their home country of Azerbaijan but really shouldn't be that difficult. I mean they're Afan Lido difficult, not Manchester United difficult. This proved to be the case as the Swans ran out 3–1 winners on a not-so-easy-to-play-on bobbly pitch which caused a few concerns. I hear straight away that any other planned games such as the UAE experiment coming in a few days will not be played on the surface we used against Inter Baku. Bischofshofen is a couple of hours away and the Swans adapt well to a somewhat ill-prepared pitch. Dyer bagged one as did Scotty and Luke Moore opened his pre-season Swansea scoring account. The usual Swansea dominance paid off and the game was a bit of a lesson for Inter Baku who I would say were at best League Two standard. The woodwork took a pelting as well, and to be honest it could have been seven. Most of the squad had a run-out and fine performances from Nathan Dyer, Andrea Orlandi and Danny Graham, for me stole the headlines, not that headlines will ever be written about this game.

So the UAE game will be in Flachau, and the switch is more to do with the pitch quality than anything else. The training takes on a more fast-paced intensity as training games come thick and fast and I really do admire the manager's ethos here. No big-game Charlie teams in sight, just pure football drills and competitive games among the squad. I suppose the critics will soon be lining up if our pre-season plans are brought in to question by poor results as the season starts. However, the team look fit, healthy and happy. And that last word I think means more to Brendan than a high-profile game to keep the fans happy. Good skills.

The game against the UAE was definitely a step up, and although the Swans lost 1–0 it gave our new German trialist a chance to impress, and once again Andrea Orlandi displayed some very competent skills in a game which never really took off. Ash captained the side as once again the whole squad got a run-out. The game could have easily been won but Beattie, Dobbie, Orlandi, Ryan Harley and Tatey all missed chances. The squad looked Billy-bollocksed by the end of the game.

The plus side reveals Kemy Agustien back and looking very polished in a Swans shirt. Ryan Harley seemed to look the part as well, I just wonder if he has that cutting edge in midfield to be better than Nathan, Scotty and Joe Allen, and more so Leon Britton, Kemy and Andrea Orlandi who is impressing at the moment. It's going to be difficult for Harley to feature at all in this side in the Premier League.

I am impressed by the team's management, especially Colin Pascoe's organisational skills. There is a belief among coaches and sports scientists that we have actually gained from this experience and the two games in the next week at the Liberty will show this. Football can be an exact science, and the very carefully prescribed training sessions and competitive games so far have revealed a clever anticipation of the test to come. I suppose only time will tell but as the team return from Austria I feel a warm and comforting sense again, reassured by the manager's calm and collected exterior. Would we want anyone else?

When a team is away and out of the limelight the press, especially those who haunt the Premier League clubs, will look anywhere for stories. These usually surface in headlines about drunken behaviour or nightclub bouts of stupidity and the like. In the hideaway that was Salzburg this was never going to be the case. Not only did the club very carefully plan the training and development side of the squad's fitness improvement, they very cleverly placed the team in a position where nothing much could happen. Another chance decision? I think not. It can't all be luck. Two games now surface in far more competitive terms, Celtic and Real Betis, both top-flight teams from Scotland and Spain respectively. If there is a gauge as to Brendan's ability to plan and prepare a team for the Premier League, then it will be these two matches.

The positives so far have been Kemy back to fitness and looking silky smooth in midfield and Orlandi playing as if he has broken few of those shackles he has worn so often in recent years. Maybe he will feature more this season as he hasn't disappointed to date: he looks to be a player full of confidence, clearly displaying an ability that I really didn't know or believed he had. Credit where it is due. The friendlies are almost mouth-watering, well, -ish.

Celtic, I thought were despatched very easily, and without too much shouting. The game itself was a pleasure to watch and goals from Sinclair and Dobbie had a flavour of last season about them. Both scored together just like Wembley, and I get my first competitive glimpse of Gerhard Tremmel, signed from Red Bull Salzburg, a player even older than Moreira. His signing passed me by somewhat; after his trial I thought that would be it . . . I have been too busy watching Michel Vorm. Having said all I have about keepers, the Celtic custodian, one Domonic Cervi, needs to have a look at himself, he doesn't look happy between the sticks at all.

Tremmel gets a part to play as Celtic prove many people right in their assessment that they are merely a Championship side in skill and ability. In fact maybe I am doing the rest of the Championship a disservice – at least on this showing. Luke Moore looked tasty up front on for Nathan Dyer, and for me this season could well take his chance, if he is given it that is, to make a play for the striker's jersey. Danny Graham will take some shifting, though the amount of money paid dictates he will get first dibs on the striker's shirt. Danny looked very sharp, and as quick and agile as he did the last time he played at the Liberty, in a Watford-dominated game last season. The Celtic fans danced and sang all evening, flares (not the trousers) smoking across the away end as what I estimate as an experimental side were put to the sword. My mate back in Gloucester listened to the game on Celtic's radio station and said he had never heard such a biased load of dross in his life. I immediately asked him if he had ever read some of the more biased press we have in Wales. One game down on the two-way ticket, and the Swans win 2–0. Easy. The manager described the game as a perfect win; I am not so sure, but it was enjoyable.

A Swansea City second string drew with Afan Lido 1–1 (told you) and the players involved for me will not feature at all this season, which maybe reflected the scoreline more fairly. Tommy Butler equalised half way through the second half after a disappointing effort from the reserves saw them go one down.

Leroy Lita completed the formalities today as well, and I hear on the grapevine that we are now officially talking to Michel Vorm and one Wayne Routledge. I am marginally impressed – a few bad boys seem to be joining the ranks. Routledge took ages to complete, and Newcastle got a fair old price for him. The on-and-off deal took three hard weeks of negotiating, and credit to the Swansea board for not telling Mike Ashby to shove it up his well-upholstered backside. The only thing that bugs me is that Routledge hasn't scored in the Premier League. Yes he is an exciting player, but it's goals we need as well as all the tricks. In Vorm's case he is most welcome as an addition to the playing staff, and my very knowledgeable contacts tell me he is most definitely a class act. This will almost certainly see him cemented as Swansea' s number one. In fact when Vorm is compared by my Dutch contact in the Hague to Dorus he says quite simply 'Vorm is in a different class, you will see,' I bloody hope so. Let's get this deal done.

So we have choices now, Lita and Routledge add firepower to the midfield and attack, and with Danny Graham, our other significant signing, I am today as warm as the Swansea sun for our Real Betis test. I am confident about our early season chances. The bookies aren't though, and offer us as favourites in some cases (in every case in fact) for the drop. This is traditional for the bigger bookies; they often make all the promoted teams relegation candidates. When Blackpool started so well last season they were still odds-on for the drop, even when they were in the top six. And the bookies wouldn't be bookies if they weren't right more than they are wrong. Clouds of despair descend on me again. Bastards.

Real Betis are simply the best side we have faced so far. Tatey comes close with a firm header and Danny Graham has the ball taken off his foot early on. Betis attack quickly and effectively with Rubén Castro looking like lightning; he misses chances as does Molina and the half way mark greets us with a 0–0 scoreline. Moreira looked very capable in the first half between the sticks and then we get to see Tremmel again, and if Vorm does sign I think he could well be the back-up keeper as the season progresses. Moreira is decent but Tremmel looks a bit more reassuring. The game spun on a striker's ability to seize upon a chance and do the damage. That striker was Danny Graham, and the chance was sublime effort displaying strength and prowess to finish and put the Swans 1–0 up. The very decent crowd cheered loudly, and Danny looked most pleased with himself. Many changes took place after that, but most pleasing for all of us was the final whistle and another victory against a very decent top-flight side. Seemingly the prep and planning for these two home games before the Premier League campaign starts has been spot on, and who would have argued otherwise ?

The summer months have been hard work, June and July especially. They have been made easier by the endless speculation on who is signing for the Swans and who isn't. The fact we have spent more than £9m overall is indicative of a club which is careful still in its financial planning. They have to be, the £90m isn't here yet . . . that takes a long time to materialise. However, the board can plan, and they can see a bright future for us all surely? Then I look at those first three away fixtures . . . oh shit, oh bloody shit. Man City, Arsenal and Chelsea. Oh dear. But at least we are here, and unlike some close by, at least we haven't bottled it – again.

Chapter Four

August: Riot-Torn City

But first a lesson. The usual Swansea City rush to the line has started, and it starts with Michel Vorm signing for us as many had expected two weeks ago. The relentless speculation wasn't wrong this time and has resulted in a cracking signing for the club. In Vorm we have a real gem, a keeper who is far better than anything we have had since Roger Freestone last 'two-stepped' his way in to the number one jersey, and made it his own for years and years. Vorm is twenty-seven, and his best years are ahead of him. As a keeper he has earned the right to play for the Dutch international side and is, for me, a better, more competent footballer than Dorus de Vries. And the fee comes out in real terms at £1.6m. With Routledge already in place the club have stretched the time limits again to get in quality players at the last minute. This is a good strategy, and Swansea being *the* Premier League club means we hold many cards. The other issue will of course be demanding (and stupid) agents with deluded prices in their minds to go with the deluded rationale many have for their players, and in a few cases, and quite openly, for themselves.

Today, is the day Vorm is at Swansea. It's 6 August 2011. I spoke to a pretty well-known and fair-minded agent, and another at the end of the day who is so far out of touch with the Swansea City philosophy, he was almost the first candidate of the month for sectioning. And I do not say this lightly, he is a complete and utter buffoon.

My first agent encounter came at 10 o'clock, with a man who I have much respect for, and many know him from the television and his time as a manager. He now mentors new agents and offers advice and guidance for those newly accredited agents of tomorrow. Hence the reason I speak with him so often. What I need to get to understand is the mindset of football agents . . . those agents who are operating daily with a number of decent and well-known names on their books. What drives them, the people they work for and the overall motivation?

Yes, the word money will spring into the conversation, but there are a number of well-known agents, like my mentor, who are hardworking, honest and extremely law-abiding. Some have done the FA route to qualify as an agent, while others gain accreditation via prior training as law graduates or solicitors. Times are changing – slowly in the murky world of FA agents. My mentor speaks intelligently and thoughtfully; he is a man who has experienced the best as a player and the worst as a manager. A man with a high regard for trust and confidence, and with that in mind I will keep his confidence for the next few pages. Agents earn a lot of money, especially those who work in the higher echelons of the industry. Those who work 'for agencies' can find themselves under considerable pressure to deliver and look after the players signed to them.

Those who operate alone can be one-off agents, like those who look after 'mates from school' who make it to the big time. The player has with them someone who they trust and the agent (their mate) works closely with them for a ten-year period. These are clever moves, which mean the agent doesn't always need to qualify to become an agent to 'look after the interests' of the player. This can go unlegislated though, and bring with it a few issues, one of them being that unqualified people in contract negotiation and settlement roles can cause legal issues. They shouldn't be involved, but of course if they are offering advice, they will be by virtue of the fact they have the player's ear. There have been a number of players, including a few players at our beloved club, who maybe have been given the wrong advice at times to sign or not sign from agents who know little about our footballing philosophy and structure. This is where the money and greed comes in. The agent doesn't have any loyalty to Swansea City, and only slightly more to the player. What they have their eye on is the big money move to another club who offer more cash, but maybe not the lifestyle, social life and standing that the player would get at Swansea City. Money talks, the player walks and repents at his leisure. And in recent times I am sure we could all name a few players who fit that criteria having left the club. In fact I spoke to one the other day. He is not a happy bunny, and regrets the day he left our club. He really didn't realise just how much better off he would have been had he not left when he did. And he and his agent don't talk anymore, well they wouldn't would they? He is a non-league player now, the agent has moved on and the player no longer has any financial draw to him. Loyalty see? He really had none at all from the agent who took his 15 per cent (25 per cent for some of his deals) and walked away. Now, Swansea City may be unique. But look at Ferrie Bodde and Owain Tudor Jones. Both had very bad injuries, Swansea stuck by them and gave them all the support they needed, including the very best surgeons to fix their career-ending injuries. In Owain's case it worked, and once fixed he left the club for a small fee. The loyalty came from the club, and that is a real quality I admire now at the Liberty. That is what I want my community club run by local people to be remembered for, not demonstrations, fighting and aggression from and between fans and the club's shareholders and directors. We have been spoilt at Swansea, and many clubs need to look at what we did and how we did it.

I am getting a fuller and more experienced picture of the agents' lifestyles now and the expectations on the role itself, but I still need more time before I maybe make that move having competed all that I can for now. Then my mentor gives me a number, 'Call him and ask him about how he does things, and listen to what he says.' Later that day I had an incredible conversation with a registered football agent, who will go by the name of 'the Grouter'. I call him this not because he runs a tiling company but because in his words 'I fill in the cracks; I produce a filling that looks good and feels good. Like everything it won't last forever, but while the pound signs are in the mixing bowl, the finish looks superb.' Now that is a quality statement, and nobody can make that up.

The Grouter has been in football for years. He isn't an ex player or manager, he comes from the Stan Flashman era. He has mixed with the good, the bad and the fucking ugly in football circles. He knows everyone, and is a face which is seen and regularly noticed at games from the Conference to the Premier League. He is not a criminal, but makes things work to 'enable ' things to happen.'

He is aware of things that he maybe shouldn't be, like the contents of contracts because he knows that the standard contract will have these add-ons and common sense prevails in this arena. Everyone will have a 'buy-out' and everyone should have a time limit written in to their playing contract; many will have image rights and other add-ons as well. These things are not hard to gauge. Yes, the specifics cannot be known unless it is leaked, but a professional and experienced agent can easily work out the ins and outs, as can clubs. Now clubs, including Swansea City, employ agents as well as having to put up with them when a player signs for the club. Agents can be employed to find players and recommend players, making it easy for the club to source and analyse those available assets for sale or transfer.

Also, an agent can be told of a pending move for their player away from their contracted club by the manager or chairman, thus ensuring they get a heads up and can find another club for their asset. This means they can tout the player to other clubs, and agree an early transfer for the player and financial security for a few more years. So an agent isn't just someone who turns up with a big cigar and a flashy suit demanding a sackload of money for the player (and in turn, themselves). Agents deal with players and have a contract between themselves on an agreed percentage. The monthly salary percentage and other specific monetary deals which make the contract watertight and understandable for the player and agent are then added. Many of those contracts go through some due diligence by a third party in law, and these contracts are known by the FA. The FA also know who is owned by and who is working with whom. They do their very best to legislate this appropriately, but remember, lots of money is involved, and ownership, agents and clubs all want to make or save as much as they can. So agents are employed by clubs as well as by agencies and players, and they also canvass for work. So, there has to be a lot of monitoring by football's governing body including FIFA, and sometimes there is a huge conflict of interest.

Did you know that between 1998 and 2003 Swansea City spent £20,000 on one player, a certain Tommy Mutton, and signed thirty-four UK-based players including the likes of Leon Britton, Alan Tate, Roberto Martinez, James Thomas, John Williams and Walter Boyd (Jamaica) all for free? Clever work for the time; admittedly they were signings made initially by an owner who was looking to spend nothing and make something out of everything.

However, that is some feat. Walter Boyd came to Swansea City's attention from the usual overseas agent sending the club a video tape and making contact with the then owner via their business colleagues in London. I know this because the agent told me. The simple signing process was initiated and bang, before you know it Walter Boyd is making an impact and scoring goals for Swansea City. It was good business by people who had no money to spend, even though they said they did. The club back then had no choice but fulfil the basic demands of the fans by employing foreign agents to bring in players, and a handful of UK-based agents as well. It isn't dodgy, but that's what happened.

The same process was employed by Nick Cusack when he and Roger Freestone took over the managerial affairs at the club, and for a few years after that until we started signing the likes of Leon Knight, Darren Pratley and Rory Fallon for decent lower-league fees. This was carefully managed by the current board, and they saw quickly that a little investment could attract to the club a better squad and improved hope for the future. The board then as now had the club at heart, unlike the previous administrations – all they were interested in was their own personal gain. In fact it wasn't for two seasons of the current board being in place that Swansea City signed Paul Connor from Rochdale for a reported £35,000 – after nearly three years of careful management and stability, Swansea City felt confident enough to spend some money. Having come out of a CVA (Company Voluntary Agreement) the club couldn't go mad and spend hundreds of thousands – that would piss off the creditors who took five pence in the pound (including previous manager John Hollins who in my opinion was paid too much anyway) as a result of the CVA.

In the 2005/06 season Swansea City first started the financial rebuild by spending around £600,000 on playing staff and this coincided with the formative Liberty years for the club. It was at this time that Swansea first started to display the concept we know today as the 'Swansea way' on the pitch too. It is no coincidence that the Liberty move breathed a fresh and positive outlook in to the club and board and enabled us to look to the future without the cloud of administration hanging over us. Young supporters who came to the club at this time will know little of what happened before, but it has to be documented so history reflects a truthful account of how our club was literally saved as it drew its last breath. It was saved by love and a desire to rehabilitate and restructure an honest and trusting club, a well-thought-of set-up that embraces people and values them – and that wasn't just on the make for an individual's own good.

Only when Kenny Jackett had done all he could at League One level and was moved on (and to some extent Bryan Flynn before him), was the template ready to be moved forwards. Roberto Martinez was the man for the job according to Huw Jenkins. It was a move which I felt was so wrong that I was stunned; however, what do I know, eh? Roberto moved the club up a level, and with more investment available he managed such a revival that promotion seemed almost a given to the Swansea support. We would make the Championship, and everyone had no doubt about that. It was for me, just a case of *when* as opposed to *if*. From February 2007 to the end of that season we played eleven games and went unbeaten as a team. Cast your minds back to the Blackpool home game at the end of that season. We lost 6–3 in a game where we had to score loads. It wasn't enough of course but that game set the scene for a magnificent 2007/08 season. The style changed dramatically and players like Ashley Williams, Ferrie Bodde and Jason Scotland were filling the Swansea jerseys on the pitch, and off it the club was rising dramatically both in stock and in fanbase. It would only be a matter of months before Swansea City returned to the rightful place as Wales' top football club. Cardiff City were experiencing 8,000 crowds in the Championship rising to 11,000 on average at Ninian Park, and even though they were fighting it out in the top six of the league for a time, they would quickly fall to mid-table mediocrity yet again. The Cardiff hardcore were looking jealously behind them as the Swansea dragon was roaring in readiness to overtake them.

Swansea's arrival in the Championship came after the most successful season since the club were promoted to Division One back in the good old days of the early 1980s. They were promoted as champions, and worthy champions even though Leeds United had suffered a points deduction for irregular administration of their club. Swansea overtook the Leeds points reduction and in any event, even if Leeds had recovered all the points they were deducted, they would still have finished second to Swansea City. That's how good that season was. It was Championship form and the likes of Doncaster away were complete football displays (the side showed total domination in a 4–0 victory). It was at this time that Roberto Martinez made the famous 'I will only leave if I am forced out' statement which lulled the more gullible of fans in to a false sense of security as his achievements were being noticed at higher levels. Behind the scenes the first cracks appeared that even the Grouter (I haven't forgotten him) couldn't polish over. Martinez wanted more money and more financial support, but the board not wanting to create another CVA or be in any way involved in such a move were far more careful. Money splits the very best of relationships and after a successful first season in the Championship, Martinez was poached – maybe coaxed – but in any event left Swansea for Wigan Athletic. There he would find more support – it was his first club after all. Many Swans fans were unhappy – so unhappy in fact that Martinez needed a degree of police protection, but all the same another era had ended.

Transfers in the first season in the Championship saw a balance sheet of about £600,000 in player expenditure. Remember this was the season Lee Trundle moved for £1m to Bristol City, a move which I am sure in hindsight he regretted, but in Swansea City's case was very good business. Martinez's replacement was one Paulo Sousa, a man with a different philosophy and group mentality in his football armoury. A man also who for me had absolutely no idea about operating in the transfer market and his knowledge of players was very limited, especially those players who fitted the financial structure of Swansea City. Having said that, another top-ten finish saw the club almost in the play-offs at the end of the 2009/10 season – a seventh-place finish was commendable after so little transfer activity. In fact this season saw Swansea employ more agents than any other season, resulting in a lot of expenditure – quite a few hundreds of thousands – spent on fees to get the likes of Shefki Kuqi, Craig Beattie and Stephen Dobbie. This signalled to me an early warning that Sousa was not operating as expected. In January 2010 Sousa loaned Dobbie to Blackpool, and the brave Scot fired the goals that saw Swansea pipped to a play-off spot. This was not endearing him to the board at all. The agents' fees paid out coupled with this managerial cock-up drove a wedge between the Huw Jenkins/Sousa relationship and also saw Leon Britton leave the club for Sheffield United. Sousa left in the summer of 2010, and even though he led us to our highest league position in twenty-seven years, not many were disappointed to see him go. His season with us was uninspiring, and the football merely consolidated or should I say covered up even more cracks. Thankfully Craig Beattie didn't get a nailed-on penalty that final day of the 2009/10 season, and thankfully Swansea City didn't make the play-offs. I say that now, knowing what Sousa's replacement achieved the very next year. But Paulo Sousa did what he wanted to do, he coached us into a style of play which ensured we wouldn't get relegated, and that for him, but not for many others, was a success.

The Brendan Rodgers era then started and for all of us these recent times are well documented. However, it is this recent history that is unknown territory for the media, agents and those who know little of our club. This is where a number of negotiations will fall by the wayside, and Marcos Senna will be an example of a player looking for a big payday on the back of our club's hard work. Well that's tough mate – that just is not going to happen. What a joker.

This takes me back to the Grouter. He tells me that he sees our club as a bit of a treasure chest, a club run by non-football people (when will they be football people?). They have a limited knowledge of the Premier League and agents like Mr Grouter will prey on their weaknesses as many times and as often as he can. Huw Jenkins will know what I mean – he may even have an inkling as to who the Grouter is; they have met a few times. The last time Huw left the man in no doubt as to the Swansea City situation. You see, agents like the Grouter are merciless, they are creatures of habit, and this is their weakness. Swansea City FC will not make him welcome at the Liberty. Like a greedy little boy he will return and take advantage of a club as many times as he can, caring not for how he is perceived, and will not really care what he leaves in his wake. Yes he is a Jack, but not in Swansea terms, he is merely an 'I'm alright Jack'. That's not the same thing. I mentioned to him that he should do a little research on the club and board and understand the feeling they have for the city and the area. I went on to add that he would be distrusted as a result of not only his brash way, but his attitude and behaviour towards Welsh people and the club in general. His broad south-east accent will not go down well, he is noisy, and he is rude. Yes, he does hold a few keys, but I get the feeling the keys he has are pretty worn out, and it's only cash he's interested in. He reels out a load of names and shouts down the phone 'Who is the Swansea money man?' I laughed, he was a fucking idiot, just another person who thinks that Swansea have a wedged-up backer . . . how else would we have made it so far? I said my polite goodbyes. The man had turned out to be an idiot, a stereotypical football agent caught up in the sordid past of football agents. His speech was ridiculous, his waist too fat, and he probably had gout. I hated him. My parting shot to this individual went something like this:

'Maybe you should think twice before doing any business with the club, and anyway I don't think you have much that they want.'

He replied, 'I have nothing they want, but once I get in to them they will see me as their best friend.'

'Lovely job,' I said, 'best of luck mate.'

He was still bluffing and puffing as I ended the call by throwing the receiver into the garden. What a cunt.

Of course he was merely trying to impress me. He saw our club as a £90m cash cow and just wanted a slice of the action. I know he has never done any dealings with Swansea or the board, they wouldn't want to. And if I heard they were about to I would be the first to warn them. He was showing off, he probably does it all day every day to everyone he meets, or anyone who will listen. Trouble is I didn't want to listen. I rang my mentor later that evening and we both laughed over it together. He knew exactly what I meant when I said he wouldn't last five minutes in Wales. 'I know,' he replied 'but can you imagine him trying to?' Actually, I couldn't imagine him trying to . . . he wouldn't last a minute, let alone five.

The week would end (or start if you like) with an away game for Swansea at Manchester City. Their new signing Sergio (or Kun – careful how you say that) Agüero cost £38m, with add-ons worth more than the whole of the current Swansea City squad and our stadium. Football is mental. It's made even more needy by talent that is so over-rewarded that players like this individual will no doubt take centre stage. Sadly I hate him and his club already, and remember that's in a football hatred sort of way, nothing more. But you do need reminding at times don't you? If we get out of the Etihad without a hammering I will be happy. But for everyone who has an opinion on the game, a hammering seems to be on the cards.

Let's get on it now. We are Swansea City and we are cruising for a bruising. The Etihad looms like a golden oasis set among one of the most ridiculous settings I have seen for a long time. The community which surrounds the stadium may well be friendly and have a whole load of lovely people living among its ruins, but to me it looks like the most unwelcoming and totally unkempt rubbish tip in northern England. Harsh perhaps?

The weekend has had its Premier League start, and new boys being new boys get a whipping at Loftus Road with Pratley's Bolton hammering QPR 4–0 in the West London sunshine. It couldn't have happened to a nicer team. The opening day fixtures cannot be relied on that much and away wins for Manchester United and Wolves display normality in one case and surprise in another.

There are league debuts tonight for Steve Caulker and Danny Graham, and I am slightly surprised that Alan Tate starts as well, though I can't say too much about him owing to the fact he really does deserve his pop at the big time. I mean, if Tatey can do it for us this season in the best league in the world it says a lot about him as an individual and a player. I admire his knuckle-down spirit and out and out love for the city. Yes, even though I have my reservations about him at this level, who can deny him this great opportunity? Michel Vorm also starts, and I am really keen and hopeful that he is the quality we have all been hearing about. I am sort of happy we have José Moreira as back-up, but he looks slightly off the mark to me. It's all about holding out tonight.

The Etihad is a wonderful stadium, and so much has been lost in translation since it was built, not as a football stadium but for the Commonwealth Games. It shows that venues of this type can be utilised for football purposes. The gleaming pitch and freshly manicured grass clash with the floodlights, which are on but serving no purpose as the game gets underway. Thousands of Jacks are installed in the away trenches, noisily, excitedly and boisterously cheering on the ragged army on the pitch. The no-hopers, the abused minority, are here for the taking. Initially the tension in journo-speak was 'palpable', then we looked smooth, then silky, then we started to dominate. A few off-chances, off-cuts more like, but there is a glimmer of hope here. Stephen Dobbie has a long shot saved and Man City rattle our woodwork, then Vorm saves a few and they hit the woodwork again. Half time arrives and I have to say I am none too sure how the hell we survived all that. Man City were the better side, but the Swans looked organised; Tatey looked solid and Caulker assured. Could we hold out for another forty-five minutes?

Well, no is the answer, but although the opposition hit us with three goals in a fourteen-minute second-half spell, we continued to play, pass, move and dissect the Man City midfield and defence. It was end-to-end but it was the opposition who scored and the Swans who missed their chances and this was the difference tonight. That Agüero (son-in-law to Maradona), so brilliantly talented and dripping in style, sealed Swansea's fate on that hot summer night. And he really did a job on us. What a talent: 4–0 to Citeh.

The next day, as I write this, I could easily see a 7–0 loss, maybe more, but then again it wasn't deserved. The players I know have taken great strength from this result, not for the goals conceded but the way we conducted ourselves against the hot favourites for the title. Brendan will be buzzing this morning down at the training ground. I am also in touch with myself today, in three weeks *Swansea City 2010/11: Walking on Sunshine* comes out, and has already bust a few pre-order records.

In the press it's all about Manchester City and they celebrate the crushing of Swansea City in a 4–0 hammering. However, there are a few wiser journalists who comment that the performance of the Swans was an inspiration to other promoted teams. We are immediately compared to Blackpool, and everyone agrees we will go down – everyone that is except the Jack Army. The next two away games may be tough, but I just know we will take something from our next few home games.

There is the slightly difficult Carling Cup fixture at Shrewsbury ahead of us too. No longer are we the underdog and Brendan (and the players) will have to think very carefully about attitudes and behaviour at the new Shrewsbury stadium – any lack of discipline here and we will be hung out to dry. No room for big time Charlies at the Liberty. Everyone is talking up the Swans – the Welsh press in some quarters reluctantly so – but the more astute like Chris Wathen see a little more in the club than a Cardiff City byline.

Among all the furore of the opening fixtures Tommy Butler gets a new one-year deal. I am almost immediately given hope that my Premier League dream is not over either. If Tommy can get a deal then so can I. Of course, I jest and I take a bit of time out to analyse this latest contract offer. Tommy Butler did show a smattering of his real potential while we were in League One, but injury and – let's be honest – better players, have kept him out of the latest Swans set up. This offer is a real insight in to the mindset of Brendan Rodgers and his coaching and management team. Football is generally all about results, and of course a well-run and finely structured administration of financial affairs.

However, the group mentality that Brendan talks about so often is evident not just in the ninety minutes we see on the pitch, it is also enhanced off the pitch. I reckon 80 per cent of what a team achieves (any team, not just football) is achieved off the pitch. The time spent in training, in social activity, in groups, in bonding and just generally being together is so, so important. Psychologists will tell you that this is where the group is formed, and the adult learning concept will be enhanced. Players will find their own places within the pack. This is natural behaviour, which in my opinion was the reason why Leon Knight suffered somewhat during his time at the club. Away from that though, Butler's contract means something, and it means in my opinion that although he has spent a lot of time out of general team selection, he has not gone unnoticed by the management team. Tommy Butler, you see, is an enigma; he is the comic, the joker, the inside man who nurtures egos and cracks more jokes than most. Maybe without his knowledge at certain times, he is doing some of the manager's work for him by bonding within the splinter groups and forming relationships as a result. Each group has a niche of groups which form within it. Think about your workplace or mates as a group, then your favoured people within that pack. At work there may be a few of you who have lunch together, I will ask you this question – do you talk about others? Do you discuss the failings at work, the personalities who affect you? This causes disruption over time and personalities will clash. In most cases these feelings lie unchecked and surface in other forums, be they indirect behaviour, or ignoring the person who annoys you. Some people are too daft to see it, some people don't care, but organisations suffer greatly as a result, as do individuals. It is in fact the start of bullying, directly and indirectly. This actually happens. And it happens everywhere. Tommy Butler is a member of a lot of these niche groups within the Swansea City squad, and this allows him unique access to the gripes and strife which all groups suffer. Because he is the comedian he is able to see the good in everyone and bring about instant repair to any arguments or indifference. Not in every case, but in some. He is the player everyone likes, and many describe him as the funniest man they have ever met. This gracious testimony will allow Tommy to defuse certain instances of unfavourable conflict, and cement the relationships back together again. He has, I know, done this a few times already, and this type of player is invaluable to the team and the club. He is absolute gold dust to Brendan Rodgers. He competes well as a reserve team player too, but during the next few months when real character will be needed at times to step up to the Swansea cause, there will be many on- and off-pitch issues. Tommy will be there, the court jester at times maybe, deflecting the flak on to himself so equilibrium will be restored. The club need him so much as the season progresses.

The build-up to our first Premier League home game is very intense and the internet and media are all over it with some alarming reporting as usual from outside Wales. Without disclosing too much, some of these Fleet Street fools are a disgrace. Again, moving away from the nonsense we see the release of tickets for the Arsenal away game. This will be a fantastic trip for the Jack Army, and there will be some clamour to snap up the allocation. David Cornell, our fourth-choice keeper, has moved on to Hereford United on a season-long loan. He will find his time there very character-building as they lurch from one survival season to another. I hope he takes as much from it as he can.

Max Boyce will be singing at the Liberty prior to kick off this Saturday, cause if there is any for us to stay in the pub twenty minutes longer than usual. I didn't see him opening up the season ten years ago, and with all due respect to Max, I don't want to see him today either. These local celebs love a bit of limelight. Max is better known for supporting Wales as a nation through the medium of rugby. He has no football connections at all, and I have never heard him once come out in support of the Swans. He is generally seen clad in leeks and woolly scarves shouting 'oggy, oggy, oggy' and supporting Glyneath RFC. For some football fans Max represents the rugby fraternity that looks down on us hooligans from the Swansea North Bank. For me, I like both codes, so I don't really care. Max used to make me laugh a lot in the 1970s, before I developed a sense of humour.

Entering the stadium I feel different today, our first home game against Wigan in the Premier League with a certain Roberto

Martinez in charge. A man I never hated, why should I? He made a professional choice based on finance (like Dorus and Darren) and in there somewhere is a misguided belief that Wigan offered more than Swansea could. Well, at the time we were a Championship club and Wigan were in the Premier League and more money was available. Nowadays he looks happy enough, his hair has grown considerably and darkened somewhat strangely since those early Wigan days. So, health wise he is defeating the experts, or maybe getting help from them? Remember if you don't worship people like Martinez, then you won't be disappointed when they leave, regardless of the circumstances. You will still have your club, and the skin and bone you cherished as a god-like figure is the only thing that has gone, who should really care? Kick over the statues.

From what I have seen of Wigan they are quick and strong, and although their football style works when things are going against you, it isn't a formula that wins so many games in a row that they challenge for anything. Their style of football is backs-to-the-wall stuff, and will only prove its worth when they desperately need to win. Today they may have an extra edge to beat the Swans, with all the Martinez hype, but for me, if we play our game we will get something from the fixture.

The game was exhilarating though, and once again Michel Vorm was the star. What a find this chap is becoming, eh? He even saved a penalty as the Swans swarmed all over the Latics in a fiercely contested game. Both sides came out of it equal and with many plaudits. Ali Al Habsi is no slouch either and he denied us early on from Danny Graham and Scott Sinclair efforts. Rangel was immense pushing down the flanks in the sunshine as well; he can be a bit slow at times, but not today. Wayne Routledge looked a better option than Stephen Dobbie and opened up the Wigan defence and linked play extremely well as the Swans pressed hard for victory. It all went wrong, though, during the second half when Wigan seemed to wake up and clattered the Swansea woodwork on two occasions and then enter Jordi Gomez. In the penalty area the man that earned so many free kicks for the Swans in his time earned Wigan a penalty after an Ashley Williams challenge. Basically he dived, and the ref got blagged, but that is what he does, it's called gamesmanship or something like that.

Ben Watson stepped up to take the penalty and Michel Vorm dived to his right, the resultant save was celebrated like a goal. The game then petered out, and the Swans had earned their first point of the season in front of a sell-out home end – of course with the visitors being Wigan there was no way they were going to sell anything out. Once again Leon Britton shone in a game of could-haves, and his clear passing style has improved immensely since coming back to Swansea. I don't see him going anywhere soon again. On the point of star quality in a Swans shirt mention has to be made of Nathan Dyer, a player who is flourishing so much that I honestly believe he will be mentioned in international terms if his incredible form continues.

On a fans' note, why do people bring inflatable sheep to Swansea and wave them about? Well I know why – they are our national treasure. We love them sheeps we do, and of course we love a quick reminder to our opposition that the sheepshaggers are indeed winning. However, there has to be a limit, and at times this becomes marginally, and I say marginally, insulting. I am told that some of the Wigan fans are not that clever and I can now confirm this. This would apply to the Wigan idiot waving a plastic sheep about outside the main entrance to the stadium as I left the ground and making loud bleating noises. Then the sheep noises stopped and a very loud cheer was heard: the sheep rapidly deflated, just like the ego of this once noisy man who was now seated and rubbing his bonce.

In the aftermath of this Premier League game we journey back home to the Gloucestershire countryside, across the M4 as our resident memory man Kev (King Kev) once again entertains us with stories of Swansea long past. The opening two games have given us all a lot of hope that we can achieve 38 points by the end of next May. It's only when you look at our last two fixtures that you see an away game at Old Trafford and a home game against the once-mighty Liverpool that doubts once again begin to surface. However, it won't be our results against these sides that matter so much; surely it will be how we deal with the likes of QPR, Norwich, Sunderland (our next game) Bolton, Wolves and maybe Stoke and Blackburn which will determine the tone of our season.

For me, Norwich will present the hardest fixtures as they have a steely grit and determination at Carrow Road, and indeed they have something else forming in East Anglia which is noticeable. That noticeable thing is an attitude. Already I hear them bitching about being ignored and Swansea getting the plaudits. If I were them I would be concentrating on my own games and how they are won, not ours and how well we have started. There is always someone out there waiting to piss on your chips, and the thought of the Canaries with that ridiculous woman screaming 'let's be 'aving you!' does make me smile. In my view Norwich are looking for someone to bully. They look around and can't see anyone who fits the bill. They, like us, only have another team in blue that underachieves in their locality, and I suppose if they are looking to throw their weight around, the Swansea City support will welcome them with open arms. It will be interesting to see how they behave as the season progresses. Other people I know who genuinely follow other Premier League sides smile when Norwich are mentioned, and I am beginning to understand why.

Tickets are on sale for the Shrewsbury trip, and last-minute matters mean I can make the Carling Cup game. Hooray, but I have an unnerving feeling as I travel to the match with a freelance colleague to report on the game. I feel very nervy in fact. The Swans' support is remarkable considering the recent expense at Man City, and with big games coming up at Arsenal and Chelsea as well as the home games, there is a very big turnout from the Jacks. On the way to the game I hear that Ryan Harley (very much all of a sudden) is on his way and more than likely this will be to Brighton. I see this as a good move for him, then learn it is a permanent one. This surprises me, I thought he may well have a future with us after all we did to secure his services. However, there is more to a player than what they can give for ninety minutes on the pitch as we have already covered. Going as well, but not such a surprise, is Shaun McDonald to Bournemouth, not the country's best-kept secret.

Shaun has flattered to deceive; his past performances for Wales at Under-21 level have been excellent at times. However, in a Swans shirt he has never really excelled. Maybe he will be plying his trade at an appropriate level, but Shaun is a Jack, a true Swans fan, and I really do wish him all the very best, as many of us do. That's two players off a huge wage bill already, and a saving of around £25k a month all in. With money coming as well for both players, the club will see this as good business. Let's not keep players who we don't want to or don't fit in, and in turn give them the chance to move on elsewhere.

Brendan will make changes tonight, that's for sure. And I see Leroy Lita and Andrea Orlandi in the side alongside José Moreira between the sticks. A Premier League outfit should have the skill and craft to win this game, but have we got the desire? The Jacks are noisy and we go ahead thanks to some decent work from Orlandi and a gifted own goal from the Sheriff of Shrewsbury. Young Alfei and Walsh in the starting eleven I think is a bit of a punt by Brendan. They have a workmanlike and very keen Shrewsbury side at their throats and a wanting crowd as well. The lack of discipline spread to Tate and Williams too, and I sense my fears are being realised. I get these feelings now and again, like we all do. I had them at Nuneaton away in the FA Cup in the early 1990s when they knocked us out in extra time. That night like this the Swans are not impressing me at all. The casual stupidity of some of the passing and the nondescript football is frustrating and we pay the price. It was only a matter of time. You can't win games by virtue of who you are, nor by what you have become. Tonight we would find this out.

As the game progressed the Shrews equalised and then they took a well-deserved lead. Brendan was not happy, and for the first time since he has been with us he was displaying some slightly unnerving behaviour on the touchline. He was learning his own lesson for his selection tonight. The team looked nothing like the side from Saturday, and OK we had another Premier League home game coming up, but there could be no reason at all for this performance other than pure laziness. Being sixty-five places above a team counts for nothing in a cup tie, and history is littered with casualties of this type. As a club we have suffered a number of defeats in cup competitions to all sorts of non-league sides, and lower-league teams as well. It's time to suck it up. I want to hear what the manager really thinks, no bullshit. The final score was a 3–1 loss. After the game Brendan was clearly furious and delivered a cold and calculated summary of the reasons why. He selectively took apart the game and delivered what I wanted to hear. The truth. I am beginning to think we have been blessed with a fine football manager at last, and indeed someone who can concisely explain his feelings as well. Swansea City tonight, albeit in defeat, are extremely lucky to have him.

As you would expect from a professional manager the Shrewsbury game is done and dusted, and with no time to dwell on matters we move quickly to the home game against Sunderland. Already the press are talking about football firsts (again). We are yet to score our first goal, and we are yet to win at home, even though we have only played one game at the Liberty. The loss in the cup in midweek gets the expected response from everyone outside of the city as the manager closes the door and plots the next game, not dwelling on the past. What is sure is that Saturday's Swansea City team will look very different to the one that 'expired' in the week.

I am intrigued too that Ferrie Bodde is in and out of the country getting treatment, we all want him back and playing. Ferrie must be one of the best-treated, or maybe I should say looked-after, players in football history. His injury, now into a third season of rehabilitation, was a nasty one, but continued efforts to get him fit have failed. He cannot have too many lives left and as he gets older and his football opportunities lessen I have a degree of concern for his future. More positively Garry Monk is on the way back from his most recent injury; our club captain is also penning a few thoughts on his career for a new book next year. I hope he gets better and has more enlightened assistance than Roberto Martinez did. Roberto's book was, I have to say, truly awful. There is no excuse for all those grammatical errors and typos. Phil Sumbler and I took a bit of a roasting for Roger Freestone's biography; we were new to that type of writing, and restricted as well as to the flavour of our writing. Not an excuse, just fact. However, these things are a matter of historical fact, and they should be carefully compiled and written.

Sunderland come to the Liberty as an established and strong Premier League team. They are capable of beating anyone, and bendy-nosed manager Steve Bruce has been about a bit. In fact he is another football person best advised to stay away from the writing after his somewhat disappointing ventures in to football fiction. Alan Tate supports Sunderland and speaks proudly of his affection for the area he was brought up in. A native of Murton he states he is looking forward to playing against them. I'm not so sure that after the midweek performance in the cup he would get a game if it was down to me.

However, like you and many other Swansea City fans, I read the incompetent scribbling of an alleged professional writer, and this time it's one Mark Ryan of the *Daily Mail*. People like Ryan far too often say what they see, the bigger picture escapes them, and there is a reason for this. They haven't got the ability to look beyond themselves. After yet another 0–0 draw against Sunderland Ryan, like many others, start the nonsense we all expected. He slates Swansea because we have gone three games without a goal. This miserable piece of writing purporting to come from a journalist lays in to Brendan calling his narrative on the game nonsense. Ryan states, 'If Brendan Rodgers talks enough nonsense with confidence, everything will be all right.' Well, with only three games gone and two points gained it seems this hack just wants blood, and I personally would love to oblige him. He also has a go at the Swansea support for their chanting and support for the club and their open and vocal questioning of Mark Halsey the referee. Clearly this person is not used to passion or support, or indeed proper football. If you don't like it Ryan, do one. Honestly, you are the biggest Fleet Street fool today, and there are quite a few out there. He concludes we are in a mess already and out of the two teams battling it out today at the end of August at the Liberty only Sunderland will prosper. Well, let's see.

The fallout from Mark Ryan's piece is all over the internet with many football people surprised at such a nasty attack on a real football club. Hundreds of responses and allegations as to his newspaper's political stance are out there for all to see. Ryan continually attacked Danny Graham throughout his ill-thought-out article. This hack has personal issues against Swansea, or more than likely Welsh football in the Premier League, and they surfaced today in a belligerent and openly aggressive article on Swansea City FC. The issues are not with us, but clearly with him. But of course what better forum to air your questionable views than the *Daily Mail*, which as we all know is a newspaper designed to appeal to what type of person? Well . . . do I have to say it? You know what I mean.

The match was a bit dull at times. Tatey didn't line up against his boyhood club, as predicted. In a dull game let's not forget Scotty's drive which hit the woodwork, and some decent goalkeeping from Mignolet, another very decent stopper. John O'Shea hit the bar for the Mackems on his debut. Gyan should have scored and Vorm once again was superb. I thought Nathan could have done better in the second half, but try as he might he isn't going to be an all-out goalscorer any time soon, but what he is, really is so exciting to watch. Danny Graham, that useless striker, in the words of Ryan, missed a decent effort, but he was there to miss it. He looks as confident as he ever did at Watford. Dobbie, Lita and Allen all came on for second-half look-ins, and didn't get one, but the possession stats tell of the usual Swansea dominance. This maybe wasn't a game for the purist; it was a grafter's game, one which could have and should have gone the Swans' way. It didn't and Brendan, for all his good and well-thought-out grammar and decency needs to look at people like Ryan and give him the traditional public warning. But then I suppose he is better than that, better than a sniping little man with a grudge to bear. No, Brendan, I am very certain, will do his answering on the pitch.

Chapter Five

September:
Brand New Age

Tatey has fallen off his golf buggy! In a dramatic twist to the unconventional reasoning for being injured, Alan Tate today surfaced with one of the strangest injuries of all time. As a passenger in a golf buggy our man Tatey had his leg pinned against a tree in a bizarre accident, so the report goes. The diagnosis is a fractured tibia, and a lengthy six-month absence from the side. I feel for Tatey who has as much animosity in him for that lot down the road than most. In fact having walked the walk ('scuse the pun, Alan) through all the divisions in Jeremy Charles style, he has now got a bit of a lay-off ahead of him. I have to say I think that Neil Taylor will probably fill the left-back role this season and Rangel on the other side with Ash and Caulker in the middle of the defence. But a player like our Tatey is just what is required in the dressing room, and as able back-up coming off the bench. I'm mystified, so much so I have a closer look at the scenario presented. OK, golf buggy accident, how odd, how very, very strange. At least he got to play in the Premier League before it happened. I'm still scratching my head.

Words should be put aside as well for the reserves who play in Llanelli this season, taking Premier League football to the masses, well, at least the Scarlets down the road. Llanelli, as you would expect, is a Swansea City stronghold, taking over its love for the Swans from the Bluebirds back in the late 1970s when hundreds travelled by train into the city. The towns and villages all over South Wales are now displaying their support for the Swans, and there are even fans in the heart of Cardiff itself. It's all a part of the Premier League package. People with no axe to grind over the bitter rivalry many of us have seen and witnessed over the years will follow success. It will not matter to them where that success is, merely that it is available and ready to be followed. This is the price we pay as a Premier League club, and for me, as I have said before it's not much of a price to pay as we move ever forwards.

Reserve team manager and all round good chap Alan Curtis will preside over a number of really interesting and testing reserve games this season and his first test will be against Liverpool this week. The local press predict nearly 3,000 for the fixture. Not bad for little old Swansea, eh? I am certain that Curt will not only introduce those youngsters to the fold that need blooding but also keep the faith with the more experienced squad players like Butler, Orlandi, Gower, Beattie and Richards. This will be needed to keep a solid punch in the team when the likes of Chelsea, Liverpool, Man Utd and Blackburn (yes, they have an excellent youth set-up) all crank up the pressure.

I had a dream last night that Fede Bessone, that lurching left-back of old, had signed for us on a free from Leeds . . . then I had another dream he was interviewed as a returning Swans player at Llandarcy. Then I saw him in the new training kit. I even saw him in the club shop and buying chips in Rossi's. Now if he is in Rossi's he must have signed for us. Then I realised I was awake, I was not dreaming, and to be honest it wasn't a nightmare, it was one of those wake up laughing type slumbers. Fede left the Swans for pastures new, like many before him he went to a club that was bigger, better, more able and more capable of things than Swansea City. Then like me he also realised he was awake and not dreaming. After a terrible start at Leeds his career was going nowhere and he jumped at the chance of returning to Swansea (who went somewhere without him). Some have said this is a strange signing, but I don't; he is a player who will not even feature in the first team even when it hits crisis point. He is merely a squad player – a cheap alternative to whatever else is available this time of the season. He will do a decent job in the reserves, or on the bench at Llanelli, and for me this is again good business. Why spend money bolstering the team ad hoc, when Fede is on the radar? Gerhard Tremmel made his move permanent as well today. We have a lot of goalkeepers at the ready, but nobody will be shifting Michel Vorm any time soon.

The league table looks good from a Swans point of view. After three games we have two points, and that puts us in fifteenth, and this type of finish I predict for us come next May. Regardless of what the rest of the world thinks there are many Jacks who think the same. Liverpool lead the league on seven points, but that's not commented on at all. The Scousers, led by 'King Kenny', are expected to be in the top six. What also is expected is Blackburn at the bottom of the table. As long as Steve Kean remains at that club, that will be one relegation space filled. We just have to wish the same for Bolton, Wigan, QPR, Wolves and one from Villa or Stoke. That leaves us and the boring but highly competent Norwich to go about our business of collecting points. I introduce Stoke into the mix, not just to annoy my mate Mike from Gloucester (well, a bit), but in hope that if a team called SCFC is relegated, then it's them. Sorry mate.

The bottom three look promising. With Blackburn there are Spurs and WBA. Oh, and the Swans are above Arsenal – yes, we are in a right old pickle aren't we? Mention has to go to Man Utd and their 8–2 win over the Gunners, probably already the performance of the season. If that were Swansea it would be expected, but it was Arsenal, and their supporters immediately call for the manager's head and for their board to spend a £100m on new players. As I said earlier on – idiots. If you ever hear a Swans fan saying this remove them from the building. The Swans reserves beat Liverpool 2–1 as well.

What is lovely to see is the likes of Steve Caulker playing for the England Under-21s, and Scott getting in to the mix as well, as a Swans international shows we are not exactly being ignored by Stuart Pearce. I mean after all as I glanced to my left at a recent concert, and as the sweat poured down my face, Stuart Pearce was there with beaming smile just loving the noise. Now how can I have a go at him? The man obviously has very good musical taste.

The international break also brings with it Welsh games and four Swans get into the U-21s: they are Daniel Alfei, Jazz Richards, Lee Lucas and Ben Davies. I was recently asked why the Swans don't bring on young players . . . well, do I really have to answer them? Add Ashley Williams, Neil Taylor and Joe Allen to the full side and all of a sudden the training ground is pretty quiet this week. A 2–1 win for the senior side against Montenegro brings a welcome first victory for Gary Speed, a manager who is slowly embracing the Swansea way and veering away from the capital city influence. This is pleasing, if Gary can get the guys playing with half the ability he had as a player then the future is bright for the national side. Tonight I saw glimpses of a team having come out of its transformation and moving into a new gear. A brand new age is indeed just around the corner. This is further on display as the side go down narrowly at Wembley to England 1–0. Outside a Welsh supporter lost his life in a fight with other Welsh fans. Arrests were made, and the nature of the incident clouds any progress the national side is making on the pitch. The death is so shocking I take a day out to think about this football nonsense. Utter madness.

The death of Mike Dye at Wembley, an avid Cardiff fan, has shocked me to the core. As a fan I know his emotions, his anger and passion, albeit from a few miles east. There are few differences in South Wales, the people and the culture. Then another death is announced. Brendan Rodgers' father has lost his fight against cancer and died on the morning of the Arsenal away game. Brendan wants to be with his family, and the club rightly grant any wish they can to him. With all that has gone on in his private life, Brendan continues to conduct himself professionally on behalf of our club, right up to the last minute. Behind the scenes he has had to manage a Premier League football club, mourn the death of his mother and now his father, keep his family strong and nurture their love and support – all in a twelve-month period. To remain so conscious and clear even when the press vultures are starting to gather, uncaring about how he is perceived, tells me that this man, Brendan Rodgers, has more about him than most men who have tried and failed. And in that statement I include those who have succeeded and achieved at the very height of their profession as well. He walks equal to all men today, but there is a difference, he walks tall and with dignity in moments of despair. These are qualities not often found in many leaders, because many leaders don't have the qualities of Brendan Rodgers.

Deadline day also brings with it the signing of Darnel Situ from Lens in France, definitely one for the future as the Swans now build with not only one eye on next season but for seasons to come. Brendan also has other irons in the fire across the water and in Scotland. With this confidence and ability at the helm I too feel very confident that we are going in the right direction. I have no doubt that now we have the financial ability off the pitch that the manager will also be well-supported by the board and Martin Morgan as the season moves forwards. Bloody hell are we the luckiest fans in the world? I think we are.

There is now an unstoppable army on the move, it's the sell-out away support for the Swans' visit to the Emirates. The place where the lookie-likeys hang about on those vast Emirates steps. John Lydon is a supporter, and that gives the Arsenal a bit of kudos, but as soon as you see the place and the many, many doppelgangers outside, dripping in pretend gold with odd haircuts like the players they foolishly worship, I think to myself 'I hope we smash you to pieces today'. The fact that Arsenal lost their last game 8–2 is a slight worry, they might come out all guns blazing and take little Swansea to the cleaners. It was only a few months ago they did the same to Barcelona and they aren't a bad side on their day. I say that as Arsenal, like Barca and Swansea have a total football philosophy. It is slowly being mentioned in certain quarters (and should you wish to listen) that the Swans' style of play is a native version of the Barca team play and craft. OK, if that's what you want let's see how today goes.

Today will all be about Arsenal and the comeback from a terrible defeat up north. The London hacks are going to be at the ready with their football reports that will be littered with ignorance again, of this I have no doubt. I may sound bitter, but, for me, if you're going to write something at least have the nous to research it properly. The game was a revelation for us all. I will get it out of the way quickly – Arsenal won 1–0 – and the reason was a very strange (not golf buggy strange, but almost) situation which Michel Vorm instigated. Throwing the ball to Àngel Rangel it bounced back off the defender's leg for Arshavin to slot home what would be the winner. Before and after that we excelled with an organised display that was ultra-competent, and Scott Sinclair, once again, hit the bar from a shot but it was Danny Graham I felt sorry for. His confidence is still sky-high, and having made the run to get in to position for a decent cross from Agustien, his shot was very well saved by Szczesny. Caulker cleared off the line and got injured, and unusually for the Swans two bookings were received. One for Caulker, and as a Tottenham player returning to wrong side of North London that's a given, and Agustien got one as well. The fair play league takes a hit. All subs were used again by the stand-in manager Colin Pascoe, with Luke Moore, Stephen Dobbie and Mark Gower (another ex-Spurs man) making appearances. All displayed a thorough and competent knowledge of the Swans' gameplan, and I was very disappointed to see us lose the game. Again we take great heart from this match, and it really is only a matter of time before the hacks, journos and so-called experts get a dose of Jack – rammed down their throats.

Keeping an eye on the main papers this week it's David Hytner of the *Guardian* who leads us through the game the next day. His report is all Arsenal, all about the London team and finishes with one paragraph on the Swans. Well, I suppose that's an improvement; if you don't know one of the teams involved, then don't mention them. And anyway, it's Arsenal that are important, Arteta making his debut, excuses for Ramsey and let's not forget van Persie's shot that hit the post. All in all a worthy weekend in London for the Swans and still, we are not in the relegation placings – we are close, but not in there, not yet.

Manchester United continue to set fire to teams and this time they beat Bolton 5–0 away. The Red Devils are in scintillating form at the moment. Seemingly unstoppable they are joined on twelve points by Manchester City, a team for me assembled as a result of too much money, not as a result of careful planning and good managerial decision-making. I reckon both me and you could stand there on the touchline with a pale blue scarf on and lead them to some sort of glory. I suppose if Man City do win something this season then the fans at the Etihad will take it like many fans would, with a few days of celebration. For me, this is not a victory, buying a club then spending £300m on players is a false gesture, a meaningless victory, a hollow victory. Like Chelsea this is meaningless, and I would hate to support these teams. If you said to me now 'I bet you would love that to happen to Swansea,' I would have to say 'I don't think so,' because as soon as I sniff that type of club owners at Swansea City AFC, I would seriously have to evaluate how I feel about continuing my support for them. We didn't fight like demons, and nearly lose everything for our club to become the very thing all football fans should hate – not celebrate. There is always Gloucester City.

I'll be honest, I couldn't think of a life without Swansea City FC, but then again I couldn't think of a life without a lot of things.

The mining tragedy at Gleision Colliery, Pontardawe, sees four Swansea Valley miners killed at work, and once again we are reminded just how fragile it all is when four brave hard working men at a community mine lose their lives. This Saturday the club will hold a silence before the game starts and it goes without saying that we all expect both sets of fans to observe the mark of respect. Huw Jenkins carries himself incredibly well in the media, finding himself in the spotlight again for tragic reasons. We have had far too many in recent weeks.

In a list of football firsts this season the first thing we need to do is score goals. Goals have proved hard to come by, and the person getting the brunt of the grief is our £3.5m striker, Danny Graham. After four games and a number of attempts Danny has threatened to score every fifteen minutes, but to date he has not bagged one. But I reckon things will change this Saturday. Home to West Brom is for me an easier fixture to navigate and this is Swansea City's opportunity to bring about some real responses to the criticism they have been receiving and the only way to shut a few mouths legally is to score some goals.

The journey to Swansea is an uneventful one and the usual Rossi's chip shop stopover has been replaced almost permanently now by a trip to the Globe just at the back of beyond and round the corner from sideways. It's a great pub, and securing a table does require a degree of timeliness, which to date has not been a problem. I expect as the bigger games and indeed the Sunday kick-offs appear this will have to be revisited. For now, safely ensconced in the pub, talk turns to the team selection and who will be in the starting eleven. I get a nod that Leroy Lita may well appear up front, and it's not a bad shout; he will need to take his opportunity because next week its Chelsea away, and lets be fair, that's a home banker.

As we venture towards the Liberty King Kev comes up with a fantastic 'Did you know?' question. It had me stumped and I went for Jimmy Loveridge as the answer. So what was the question? Quite simply which Swansea City player scored the club's last top-flight goal? Howard grumbled a bit and said 'Latchford' and I said he couldn't have, to which Howard replied, 'He did.' And he was right. It was twenty-eight years ago against Manchester United away in a 2–1 defeat the year the Swans were relegated. Now that is a long while to wait for a bus.

The starting eleven displays Brendan's desire to win this game at all costs. Steve Caulker is out and Garry Monk is in. Caulker is injured and Danny Graham is nowhere to be seen. A foot injury may well be the reason. I expected Rafik Halliche (a very late loan signing from Fulham) and Darnel Situ (an even later signing) to play at some point this month. They obviously have been signed to strengthen matters at the back, however neither will feature at all. That old fax machine got a dose of Robin Sharpitis at the Liberty and FIFA stopped the paperwork based on it being submitted too late. Today's football transfers have a new transfer matching system, and if lateness is not the real reason, maybe matching details have again caused an issue? Either way, this should not be happening at our club. These are the things which can change our season; we need to be professional throughout the club's structure, not caught up in a dismal past of repeating the same errors. There are people out there who for a small fee get these things sorted effectively as I have already said. It may well be that this was no fault of the club at all. Whatever the reason it mustn't happen again.

So as identified through other channels Leroy Lita starts and Luke Moore is his back-up on the bench. The midfield has Mark Gower in with Joe and Leon and then of course the usual wingers in Nathan and Scott supplying Lita with lots of ammunition (I hope). Fede appears on the bench and Lee Lucas features there too, fantastic experience for the youngster. It's an attacking side which straight away pushes the Baggies about, tugging them and pulling them everywhere. WBA looked totally demoralised and with such intricate passing the birth of the 'Swansea Triangle' is witnessed by another home sell-out crowd. It was a stylish performance which will make the Premier League sit up and take notice. Joe Allen ripped the Baggies to pieces time and time again as did Leon with probing passes which eventually snapped the resolve of our visitors. In the end Joe was upended in the penalty area by a rough tackle from Paul Scharner, a man totally out of his depth as the flying Swans swamped him, Dawson and Olsson leaving them looking ragged, ruined and out for the count. Sinclair scored the penalty, at last 1–0.

Nearly 400 minutes in coming that goal was. Of course, King Kev would tell you that it was twenty-eight years. Although Shane Long missed a sitter when Neil Taylor set him up with an awful back-pass, the game seemed to be moving in our direction. From a corner, what looked like a training ground move saw Leroy rise at the back post from a Scott Sinclair flick-on and nail the second goal of the day. He roared off, shirt waving above his head, masculine frame for all to see. That would be a booking from referee Martin Atkinson. I am told the reason is a cultural one; that players who take their tops off should be aware that the world game is broadcast across all divides and countries. Taking your shirt off offends in certain countries, and that is why the card will be yellow. You can't offend countries who pay their wedge for the screening of Premier League matches.

2–0 up and the game is surely ours, the points are most welcome, three lovely points to add to the two already gained. Ash seemed to handball, but thankfully the ref disagreed, and even though Chris Brunt scored what looked like a decent goal it was cancelled out, rightfully on examination, for offside. WBA did not come to make up the numbers and tried to bully the Swans and eventually their hard tackling and total lack of control saw Neil Taylor stretchered off after a Peter Odemwingie challenge. Fede replaced him, and I was nervous again. I shouldn't have been though because Taylor's absence for the last five minutes coupled with a busy Luke Moore who replaced Lita and Routledge replacing Dyer saw Joe score a third. West Brom may well feel a bit peeved with the result but I was peeved at Arsenal and after the home draws against Sunderland and Wigan. Swings and roundabouts. And we are on the big boys' swings tonight. *Match of the Day* will be an easier watch with that warm glow we all get from a winning weekend. And I will give the noisy Baggies who entered the ground shouting while the minute's silence was being observed a degree of flexibility. Pissed and shouting is fine I suppose, but someone should have told them that those of us who were sober and respectful were paying our respects to the dead after a tragedy in the Swansea Valley. Their behaviour thereafter, goading and beckoning the Swansea support to fight, was unacceptable.

Luckily Taylor's injury is not as bad as we all first thought, so much so he will be training again in 48 hours. Nice one Neil, you have made an exceptional start to your Premier League career. An incredible lunch time game at Blackburn gives the home side hope as they beat Arsenal 4–3, and Blackburn show a lot of spirit. I hope that dissolves before we travel there. Spurs stuff Liverpool who are showing what most people knew – they aren't good enough for any title challenge – and QPR win 3–0 at Wolves who are already looking wobbly. Joey Barton, convicted felon and all round victim, wound everyone up including the fans, the opposition and his own team at

Molineux. Apparently QPR are stupid enough to pay him £70,000 a week – surely not? I am afraid it's true. They do, and this for me just endorses his behaviour, and rewards him for being a total nutter. There was a time the game bred real characters, hard men like Ron Harris and Dave Mackay. I would have loved Joey going head to head with either of them, or maybe Johnny Giles? I imagine Joey will have his quotes book out tonight on Twitter, as one more astute journalist said, 'Quoting other people's remarks on Twitter doesn't mean you are a genius Joey, it just proves you can read.' Genius.

Swansea City are twelfth tonight, still relegation fodder apparently.

Steven Caulker will need a small knee op after banging his leg against the Emirates post which kept him out of the team last Saturday, our first win. Man Utd are looking unstoppable and I watch their crushing defeat of Chelsea, and hope (I know) Brendan is seeing the frailties I can see. Of course he is, and lots more too, I am sure. I am now filled with hope as the game on Saturday at Stamford Bridge presents an opportunity for the Swans to maybe make their knockers take note a bit more. Everyone is predicting a Chelsea victory, and I cannot disagree with that. I mean, who do we think we are believing we are good enough to beat Chelsea on their home turf?

Of course the experts are right again and sadly it was a game I could only watch from afar as the Swans lost in a hard-fought competitive match in south-west London. Fernando Torres gets his marching orders for a frustrated lunge at Mark Gower but the Swans are sunk in front of one hell of a noisy away support. Trouble flares up as well in true Chelsea v Swansea style outside the ground. Just like it always does when our two teams meet. Losing 4–1 in a game that didn't have 4–1 written on it is hard to take, but Ash did look well pleased netting with a very decent header in front of the Swansea support. Torres scored before he left the fray, and Nathan Dyer partook of the usual customary bar-hitting exercise. The performance in Brendan's words was pleasing, and he fully accepts that Torres is not a malicious player. We all accept that Chelsea deserved all three points because it is their divine right to have them. Well done.

The *Telegraph*'s Ben Findon makes the usual mistake that his peers make and talks about Chelsea and only Chelsea in his match report, and the template of giving Swansea a paragraph at the end of his report is there for all to see. OK, I am a bit bitter today –

sorry Ben, you're probably a really nice parochial writer – I didn't see us losing 4–1 to Chelsea, and get as frustrated as Torres when these things happen. The high of last week's hammering of WBA is clouded somewhat by late Chelsea goals and Leroy and Nathan missing good opportunities. Still, we are sixteenth tonight with Fulham, Blackburn, West Brom and Bolton beneath us. I wouldn't have had Fulham down there and fighting relegation this season but maybe that's OK for us as they are on Swansea's radar very shortly at the Liberty. It is a case of being content with what we have, and what we have at the end of September is a position in the Premier League that if this was the month of May would mean we had survived our first season when all predicted we would not. For small mercies we have to be grateful.

Chapter Six

October:
New Barbarians

A chap called Zoltan Liptak, once of Videoton, is running around Llandarcy this morning, a fairly windy October day trying to impress anyone who will watch. I can't see him being the answer to any professional football problem. I am reliably told he more than likely will only earn himself a nod and directions out of Wales when his trial is finished. You either see him as a twenty-six-year-old Hungarian international recently named in the best eleven players of recent Hungarian times, or a player who has had previous loans at Southend and Stevenage Borough having failed to impress at Southampton. It's hard to get excited at this latest effort to smooth over the loss of Situ and more importantly the Fulham loan signing, however, it does also show a club willing to look everywhere for the best, most available and least expensive talent. And that has long been our ethos, since 2002 in fact. These things happen for a reason, I just hope the reason has been sorted out.

It's great when the games come weekend after weekend with the odd midweek fixture thrown in as well. I don't know about you but I am no big fan of the weekend off for international games, and with a few out of the way we will enjoy our next match against Stoke because there is another international break on the way. Pointless. Garry Monk is confident we can give the Potters a bit of a lesson in manners. They do have a ruthless streak which surfaces now and again, and certain players who get under your skin a bit. But that is their way. They kick and hoof and run and engage head-on wherever possible – that is their 'A game'. They deal in immediate contact with a high-energy pulse that races throughout the team. Manager Tony Pulis has risen through the ranks of the game with the odd issue as well, and I remember well his time at Gillingham. As do most. This is where he faltered, but ended up back on top at Stoke. Both are well suited; he drives his players forwards with a style of play often criticised by fans and the media, and if the media don't like them, that means I do. So fuck 'em. They have a giraffe up front as well, one Peter Crouch, who is rubbish with the odd display of utter brilliance. When he is on his game he is unplayable. His missus is one Abbey Clancy, who for me sums up everything which is bad about so called 'celebrity' and the lengths some people will go to to avoid having a proper job. Stoke City also have Jermaine Pennant who drinks and drives, and Ricardo Fuller who likes to be arrested too. Their fans also like getting arrested and no doubt they will endear themselves to us immediately. Having said all that my good mate Mike Jennings, a confirmed Stoke supporter, is down for the day with his wife Kate and son who I meet outside Rossi's for a few chips and a nice piece of fish. Unlike Ryan Shawcross, Mike won't break your leg for supporting a different team than him. The pub is visited as well, and Mike tells me he isn't confident about the game at all today. I have to agree with him. Up there in Staffordshire next year it will be different, I will have the same feeling as he has today no doubt. But today, I just feel it is going to go our way. It has to – we need these games to be points in the bag.

Outside a few Stoke fans (in the safety of the away confines) sang 'Where's your miners gone?' and then broadcast it on YouTube while security just stood and watched them. This amazed me. I am sure if you or I were to stupidly (and I am not condoning this, it is merely an example) do the same at Liverpool regards Hillsborough, you would be up before the beak damned quickly, and rightly so, but not in Swansea it seems. This completely appals me. Maybe the stewards were too thick to notice? That angered me massively, and made me want these Potters stuffed and sent home in disgrace. Which, I am very pleased to report is just what happened. I have to say our home performances are getting better and better. They are just oozing class at the moment. The day before Man City had won 4–0 at Blackburn and Liverpool had secured the points at Goodison in the Merseyside derby. So we need to buck up and move on ourselves as well if we are to win the title. Well, you know what I mean, three points are essential. With Norwich also messing up this Sunday fixture was a must-win to keep the confidence, at least at home, at a premium. I had to laugh, though, because the opposition hit the post, and this is fast becoming a weekly occurrence, in fact the woodwork has been hit in every game we have played so far. It's a sign of the attacking style we bring to every game we play. And that's a good point as well, we do go out and try to win every game, no holds barred.

Somewhat surprisingly it was the aforementioned Ryan Shawcross who gave us our first goal when he brought down Routledge in the penalty area for a clear spot-kick. Scott Sinclair obliged and bang it's 1–0. 'He's Scotty Sinclair, He's Scotty Sinclair' the East Stand sing, with other words added about Rosie Webster, Sally and the art of lovemaking in 2011. No hair though. It was again a very watchable and fantastic performance from the Swans. The triangles were everywhere, pass, move, pass, move, triangle, triangle, pass, move. It was like watching magicians. Joe Allen once again tormented and tore the opposition to pieces, surely any coach or manager would want him in their team on this form? He has taken to the Premier League like I and many others expected and is again wonderful to watch. Referee Jones allowed the play to move along without too many stops, and well, he couldn't really stop anything because Stoke couldn't get near the ball. They were completely outclassed. Jonathan Woodgate was once, I am told, a decent player, before his . . . problems. Well, I don't think so, and why he is still playing Premier League football is beyond me – he looks like a lost soul. What a truly awful footballer, and to think they pay him as well? Unless of course Allen, Routledge (in for Britton) and Gower (never thought I would say this) are so masterful to the extent he is being outclassed? Rory Delap and Jon Walters are non-existent, and I am told by Stoke fans more informed than I that Delap is also a hopeless case and not worthy of their stripy shirt thingy they wear.

Then it happened.

Cynical challenges (being the Stoke City forte) would again be their undoing on a fairly warm Sunday afternoon west of most places. Jermaine Pennant (you would have thought he would be used to walking) strolled into Scott Sinclair and brought him down. He gets a yellow card (another let-off). This spurred on the Swans and a loose ball was latched onto by Danny Graham, who with complete composure looked up and slotted the ball away. The goal was celebrated far more than if any other player would have scored it. Danny sticks his thumb on his nose and runs to the crowd who receive him gladly. The relief on all the players' faces tells a real story. Danny had broken his duck, and the rest of the Premier League had better watch out. 2–0 to the Jacks. Perfect. Lita came on as did Luke Moore and a further goal was nearly added, but it was as predicted, Swansea City's day. A perfect day. And Stoke are indeed packed off home to wonder what it was all about. Their combative style didn't work. They picked up five bookings and got stuffed. Fair play boys.

I am very pleased to also report that Fulham beat QPR 6–0 at Craven Cottage, a wonderful scoreline. This put the weekend's results bang in our favour as does Chelsea's 5–1 win at the Reebok Stadium in Bolton. First class stuff. Tottenham beat Arsenal which all means we are sound as a pound in tenth place. Both the Manchester clubs are fighting it out at the top and at the bottom Wigan, Blackburn and Bolton, all my tips for the drop, are bang at it in an early relegation scrap. I know Wolves are also going to push it close this year along with QPR, but these are my three predictions (though I am entitled to change my mind, you know). What a lovely feeling.

Kurtis March is also celebrating this week, he scored the equaliser as Alan Curtis's reserve side took a well-earned point off Arsenal in London.

By mid-October Joe, Ash and Neil are all in the Welsh squad and training at the Liberty as Gary Speed looks really confident and oozes self-belief prior to the national side's games against Switzerland and Bulgaria. This for me will be the springboard for better things for the World Cup qualifiers. OK – 1958, give it a break, it was only eight years later that England mugged the ref and strangely won the World Cup! Not surprisingly Switzerland are despatched easily at the Liberty, Swansea once again getting the cheap international fixture. And the Swansea squad get a run out at Llanelli in a friendly which is won 3–0. This tells me more than anything that any mid-season or winter break would be complimented with all manner of fixtures and bigger clubs playing abroad in big-money games. Let's keep it as it is, we have enough time off in football, I just wish I did as well.

Well, well, well it seems Sky have worked out where the Liberty Stadium is at last and a few games get the nod for LIVE television.

OK, so they can't show Arsenal, Man Utd and City every week, but they give it a damned good go. The home game once scheduled for Boxing Day (I have that day off so I can go – it's tricky at Christmas) is moved (so I can't). Well, I say I can't . . . it just means I have to move things about a bit. But at the moment I can't, so I will need family favours, early starts and extra time to make the game. Luckily I have some thoughtful close family and an even more co-operative wife and daughters. Fucking Sky. The game is scheduled for a very convenient 5.00 p.m. kick off on the bank holiday day of 27 December. The next day most people get back to work, or some . . . like me. So I won't be back in Cardiff to pick the family up till eight o'clock, then a drive to Gloucester. That my friends is a ball ache. But an achievable ball ache all the same.

The phone crackles into life and an old writer mate who supports Naaaarwcih City is there. 'Are you coming to the game mate?'

'No.'

'Awwww why nart?, It's all on me matey.'

'No.'

'All roight then, Keef. Oil bid ye a good 'un.'

'OK. Bye.'

You see I was never going to go to this game. I had just come back from Norwich with the band having played a number of shows in Hull, London and Carlisle, so I wanted a day or two off. I had a way of watching it anyway, through a mate of a mate (through a bloody big dish) and also the thought of that long journey, even from Gloucester, didn't appeal to me. I have done it a few times before, and each time it has been a pain in the hoover. So, I am going plastic this weekend, and won't be going.

Watching the game on Arabian Nights TV with a mate called Wolfie, his dog and a bloke who continuously eats bananas and texts religously is interesting, off-putting and in the end a decent enough reason to make a quick exit with five minutes to go. I am now as bad as those supporters who leave games early. But I had a good reason. Bananaman has recently had installed the biggest fucking dish I have ever seen in his house not far from junction 12 of the M5. You can see it from the moon, the motorway and – judging by his neighbours – Asda as well. There was the constant yapping of his dog, his neighbours' dogs, the shouting from the road, the drunk man lying down opposite in his garden and the three police cars at a domestic dispute nearby.

The icing on the banana though had to be the caller at around the 85-minute mark of the game. I had sort of given up after a decent display in the second half, and Norwich seemed value for their 3–1 lead. It was a similar game to last season at their place. Bloody frustrating. The Canaries had taken a deserved lead after about 50 seconds and not long after it was 2–0. Shortly after that (the now-prolific) Danny Graham bagged one back and it was game on. We huffed and puffed a bit and the second half I felt was ours. It was just that we didn't take the chances we made and then Norwich made it 3–1 with about half an hour to go. It was at this point I took a little bit more notice of Bananaman and the goings on outside. As I said, I will do anything for the Swans – even reside for a few hours with lunatics. Then this happened.

A knock on the door. No response from Bananaman.

Another knock. Still no response.

'Er mate, the door,' I pointed to his front door.

'Nah, I'm not answering it, I don't know who it is.'

Now I don't know about you, but I am not too good at seeing through solid doors either, so I felt it necessary to look out of the window. I think it's true to say Biffa Bacon's mum was outside.

'There's a fairly large lady at the door, mate.'

He immediately looked terrified. Wolfie's dog gulped and for a moment it felt as if the world had stopped.

'Don't let her in!' he shouted.

'I don't intend to, mate – it's your house!'

'Quick! out the back way!' he shouted as he ran out of the back door. SLAM! I looked at Wolfie, Wolfie looked at me, his dog gulped and the front door came crashing in.

'Where is the cunt?' She looked even larger in the same room.

'Who?' I replied

'You fucking knows who, dickhead. Where is he or I will start smashing the place up?'

Feeling somewhat cornered (and to be honest Dobbie had come on as sub and nearly scored), I said 'He ran out the back.' Off she went shouting and I do believe (from the cabbage-like smell) expelling a fair amount of air in pursuit of Bananaman.

I asked my mate who the hell that was as the 86th minute ticked over, and we left. 'Oh, that's his missus. They are going through a bit of bother,' he replied. I spent the next few minutes contemplating her being a figure of any desire, and all I could recall was that sweet smell of odious sweat from one of her many arm pits, the tats, her yellow teeth, potentially 30-stone frame and that malodorous country smell which emanated from her rear end like a cow's guff.

'He actually slept with her?' I asked.

Wolfie halted. 'Stop it mate, you're making me feel sick.' And then, as if on cue, his dog barfed all over the floor, and most of it contained banana skins.

There is a moral to this story. If you receive the offer of a free day out and hospitality at a football match, no matter how unattractive the thought, remember – there could well be worse waiting for you round the corner. Or in Bananaman's case, behind the door. I think enough has been said about our 3–1 away loss at Norwich City. Suffice to say I expected us to lose, and lose we did.

Man City are now looking very good with a superb 4–1 win over Villa, and the Midlands club are looking extremely fragile as the season starts to take shape. We all know it takes a good eight games to establish the Premier League course for the season, however, that established relegation dogfight or promotion battle does have its upsets. The people upset at the moment are the so called experts and pundits who mouthed-off their predictions for the future two months ago. Among the worst culprits are the ex-players. They had limited intelligence on the pitch, so why then would we ever want to take any notice of them now they infest our TV screens? Mark Lawrenson made the error way back in the mid-1990s when he appallingly ridiculed Swansea City on the TV telling Jan Molby not to go anywhere near the place. This came at a time when the club needed support, not pompous prophecies from the likes of him.

These predictions, like the bookies' nailed-on certainties, are evident throughout the season. Apparently this weekend's derby game at Old Trafford is a 'title decider'. How ridiculous. The Utd v City game gives the winner three points, as does any game that is won in the Premier League. Our mighty Swans travel to Molineux for a tricky game against a Wolves team fighting off the pitch to survive as well as on it. On the pitch they have been awesome and at the same time appalling. Which team or mixture will we see for the live Sky game this Saturday?

Any trip to Wolves, even these days, comes with a few health warnings. In the main the supporters are fine, but unfortunately like our more 'energetic' supporters, there is an unruly element which to me looks a little more than a minority when it clashes with authority. Old visits to this stadium, the subway attacks and full-frontal assaults are pretty much in the past. My last trip here for a midweek game was a few seasons back when Mark Gower rattled the crossbar from 30 yards. The visit was mainly OK, but outside afterwards there was an element searching out rival fans to intimidate and fight, and both of these factions eventually found each other, leaving our weary crew to their own devices to locate cars and get onto the M5 for home.

Wolves are in a mess; the fans hate them and the players are getting booed continuously game after game. They also have a very noisy and passionate support at home when the going gets good and there is a glimmer of hope. The Swans can quickly stamp their authority on this game by bringing a few triangles with them. As Frank Burrows used to say to the team when he was manager, 'Pass the ball to someone you travelled with on the bus.' Enlightening football theory? Not really, but the Swans pass-and-move is built on this simple mantra, a mantra probably needed more for the likes of Torpey and Harris than it is for Britton and Allen. We get the early kick-off slot on Sky, and travel with a team high in confidence and very much focussed on a win; Brendan knows this. We have sneaked in a new signing in the form of Vangelis Moras, a player who featured in the 2010 World Cup for Greece. My more esteemed contacts are slightly baffled by this signing, at thirty years of age he is fine but his form is not good and he hasn't threatened any type of inclusion in a top-flight side for a few years. I remain to be convinced, but his signing again shows a degree of 'being careful' by the board, while at the same time filling in an extra space in the squad of twenty-five. He is merely cover for Garry Monk or Ashley Williams; well, at least I suppose he is, and his three-month loan will be interesting to monitor.

...ll kicks off in Manchester and the Swans are back representing Wales in the big ...gue again. Can you feel that jealous gaze from the east?
...urtesy of Matt Parry)

...game itself displayed to the nation the Swansea way, the Swansea brand and ...Swansea mentality. (Courtesy of www.swanseacity.net and Dimitri Legakis)

Olympian Joe Allen from Narberth, Pembrokeshire, in action at the Etihad. He would go on to be pivotal to the club in the Premier League – and then his country, and then his nation. . . (Courtesy of www.swanseacity.net and Dimitri Legakis)

As the season moved on the media talked of triangles, methodology and mindset trying to repeat and understand Brendan Rodgers. They knew nothing, and the r philosophy is here in this picture. Pure teamwork, pure joy, pure desire – that's t Swansea way. (Courtesy of www.swanseacity.net and Dimitri Legakis)

November Manchester United turned up at the Liberty and managed 3 points in
a game they should never have won (1–0). Scott Sinclair missed a sitter by his
standards and Alex Ferguson breathed a huge sigh of relief in his post-match
interview. (Courtesy of www.swanseacity.net and Dimitri Legakis)

Another Olympian, Scott Sinclair, tormented Manchester United all day.
They simply couldn't deal with him. (Courtesy of www.swanseacity.net and
Dimitri Legakis)

Danny boy scores away at Norwich. Both games between the clubs in the 2011/12 season would prove to be exciting affairs with goals, passion and plenty of incide (Courtesy of www.swanseacity.net and Dimitri Legakis)

The flags of our time. The Union flag and a Swansea flag sit proudly in the East Stand at the Liberty. (Courtesy of www.swanseacity.net and Dimitri Legakis)

tt and the Saundersfoot Jacks. (Courtesy of Matt Parry)

Swansea East Stand, waiting to welcome whoever it may be that takes to the y end at any Premier League fixture. The noise they create has been described assionate, exciting, amazing . . . and hostile. (Courtesy of www.swanseacity.net Dimitri Legakis)

Lewis Howells in the QPR mascot's kit against Swansea at Christmas. My good mate Marcus Howells from Merthyr is QPR through and through . . . and so, it seems, is his nephew. That has to be some form of torture? I'm sorry what I said about your team, mate – but in general and in football terms I have really fallen out of any love I may have had for them three seasons back. (Courtesy of www.swanseacity.net and Dimitri Legakis)

Cardigan Jacks in attendance: ready . . . aye! (Courtesy of www.swanseacity.net and Dimitri Legakis)

tale of two Scotts. One who plays for England and one who should play for *England. Location, location, location. Harry scuttled away from the Liberty* *raping a 1–1 draw, admiring the Swansea performance and conscious of the fact* *at Spurs, on New Year's Eve, could never spoil this Swansea party. (Courtesy of* *vw.swanseacity.net and Dimitri Legakis)*

ht at the back as well, Williams and Rangel were first-picks every time a Premier *gue fixture was played at the Liberty, which unlike certain other areas of Wales* *iost weeks. I'm just saying what you're thinking, folks!* *urtesy of www.swanseacity.net and Dimitri Legakis)*

The North Londoners pay Swansea a visit and here Steve Caulker wins again. The man they call RVP at Arsenal is just that – Really Very Poor. (Courtesy of www.swanseacity. net and Dimitri Legakis)

What better way to finish off Swansea City's domination of North London's finest at the Liberty . . . ? By celebrating another goal, of course. It's Swansea 3, Arsenal 2. Time for Wenger to blame the pitch, the referee, the fans, the weather, his missus, his dog, his watch, his feet, his glasses, his clothes . . . you get my drift. (Courtesy of www.swanseacity.net and Dimitri Legakis)

Chelsea game at Stamford Bridge was a difficult pill to swallow after such a tremendous performance. At the Liberty, Chelsea scraped a 94th-minute draw. Their travelling fans celebrated like they had won the Champions League. Of course that would never happen now . . . would it?

(Courtesy of www.swanseacity.net and Dimitri Legakis)

Ángel Rangel goes in for the ball against Chelsea's Ashley Cole during the match
Stamford Bridge. (Courtesy of www.swanseacity.net and Dimitri Legakis)

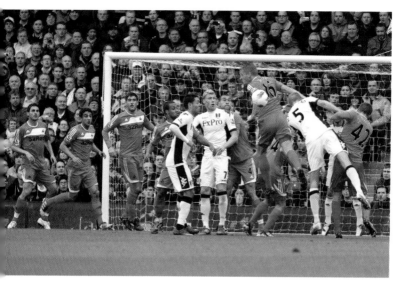

1other successful visit to West London. Fulham were despatched in what has been
scribed as the most complete Swansea City performance in years. The double
er the Cottagers is complete. It was a masterclass in passing football.
ourtesy of *www.swanseacity.net* and Dimitri Legakis)

Stephen Dobbie didn't make the impact in the Premier League we all wanted him to make. But on his umpteenth loan return to Blackpool, he once again took centre stage. (Courtesy of www.swanseacity.net and Dimitri Legakis)

Some may say it was the best home performance of the season, but all I know is that Swansea City beat the champions-in-waiting, Manchester City, at home 1–0. And fully deserved it was, too. (Courtesy of www.swanseacity.net and Dimitri Legakis)

for one and one for all. Don't complicate passion and desire. (Courtesy of w.swanseacity.net and Dimitri Legakis)

..y, goal, thumb, nose, win. (Courtesy of www.swanseacity.net and
..tri Legakis)

Apparently they call this the Poznan. The Swansea East Stand do this when they beat the team whose fans normally do the Poznan. Simple. (Courtesy of Gavin Tucker)

The players thank the fans, who thank the players, who wave at the fans, who wave at the players. Premier League football is once again a feature of Swansea City life. (Courtesy of www.swanseacity.net and Dimitri Legakis)

Now Joe Allen is talking about 'A games', which is nice to hear, because he is qualified to talk about it. He is an intelligent young man with a bright and sunny future, and that future seems to be at Swansea. I like that loyalty in a player – my club needs that. The players do get caught out now and again, and in their eagerness to please they are left somewhat wanting, especially if English is not their first language. Having said that a lot of footballers who come to our country to ply their trade seem to have mastered the mother tongue far better than some of the halfwits I see dragging themselves round my local estate. I sometimes see quotes from foreign players and actually wonder if they are actually quotes made by the player or indeed 'quotes' made by the press. Don't let the truth get in the way of a good story. Or at least make it up, it may well come true!

There are of course plus points and negative points to an early Saturday kick-off on the television. For the fan it offers a chance of an early start to the weekend, and if it is a successful one you get to wallow in the glory while others around you sweat it out for their 90 minutes. In this case today at Molineux it seems there will be no sweating, no hard fight and no hanging on at the death for the points. The Swans start in superb style, the well-oiled machine now in perfect harmony with the Brendan Rodgers Swansea City ethos. You can tell when it is going right because the home crowd go 'fucking nuts' and this is exactly what they are doing today. Apparently Wolves are playing so badly that Swansea City are making them look like fools. However, I wonder if this is really the case? Is it that Wolves are so bad, or is it that Swansea City are so good? It's a point worth pondering. The one-man team that is Scott Sinclair is now a one-man team that is Joe Allen, so let's add him to the one-man team list. Garry Monk looks so assured at the back I am wondering what all the fuss is about with Steven Caulker.

The media's search for headlines could well be cured today as Swansea City surely must take the points in Wolverhampton? If we do it will be our first away points of the season. The football is just mesmerising and I am really proud to be a Swan today. The home fans are so angry they shout continuously at manager Mick McCarthy and Swansea old boy Terry Connor genuinely looks like he is about to burst in to tears. I know that this isn't the case, it's the way he talks, but he really does have a sticky-out bottom lip

today. He is suffering as much as McCarthy is, that's for sure. Then
– bang! – goal! Danny Graham gets his third goal in three games;
this is looking so good. The crowd's hostility gets more intense, and
it increases tenfold as a twenty-eight-pass-move ends in a Swansea
City goal from Joe Allen. This is championship form, and by that I
mean championship as in the Premier League Championship. It's as
simple as that. What a half. That last goal was as good as you will
see anywhere in Europe this weekend.

At half time Brendan clearly turned all the taps off and decided
the game was won. When he talks about learning curves this game
will most certainly feature prominently in his mind. For whatever
reason we became big-game Charlies. I've seen this happen before
– when we are playing so well that we think it's a breeze – and it's
happening again. No longer is possession key and although we are
creating chances it isn't looking favourable. Sinclair is the biggest
culprit missing a few decent opportunities to put the game away.
The Wolves crowd sense something has changed as well and they
turn their negativity in to a positive roar for their team. The game is
turning and there seems to be nothing we can do. However, as time
creeps by in the second half I still have hope. The noise from the
home fans is still intense and I can't help thinking that they should
realise this more at Molineux and you never know . . . it might just
pay off on the pitch. As we progress in to the last 10 minutes the
general consensus is we have won the game, and as if to rubber-
stamp that, Brendan brings on Andrea Orlandi for Leon Britton. My
old mate reappears in a first-team strip, and straight away gives the
ball away . . . and again, and again. This weakens the midfield and
Wolves seize on that weakness to pressurise us further. As before,
I'm not happy with Orlandi. Now Nathan Dyer has run himself in
to the ground and Wayne Routledge takes his place, the thinking
behind the change being that Wayne will provide chances for us up
front and nullify this new-found spirit Wolves have fostered since
Orlandi's introduction. It doesn't work; within seconds Wolves pull
one back through Kevin Doyle and the Siege of Mafeking starts.
And fails. Within a few minutes it's 2–2 and still there is time for
more Wolves efforts to win the game. Vorm holds firm and new
signing Moras on for Gower is a lost soul in a game far beyond his
current ability.

It felt like we lost. 2–2 is the final score, and for all the chances missed, and all the comments made about our first point away from home, I am so unhappy today. This will take some getting over. I am not unhappy with any one person, although poor old Orlandi should have been better managed than to bring him on in this game – at all. And Moras was about as effective as a Roger Johnson defensive header . . . in fact that's doing Johnson an injustice.

I need to sit down for a bit before writing anymore. Maybe plant some late carrots.

I have mentioned Andrea Orlandi, and I do this because he has so much ability. The problem most Swans fans see in him is that he doesn't dominate games like he should, and again if I thought he just wasn't good enough I would say so. His standard I referred to in my last book, and that standard I think is in the region of a very good League One player. However, because he is so young, because he has the ability to improve, then Swansea City clearly see time for development.

As we move towards November the Liverpool game is taking over everybody's thoughts. Will we see a repeat of the 8–0 loss the last time we travelled to Anfield, or will we see a magnificent fighting performance that I witnessed personally back in October 1981?

Chapter Seven

November:
Wonderful Life

I suppose it's the games like Liverpool at Anfield, Manchester United at Old Trafford, etc., that will spark the fans' imagination. The huge increase in Swansea City's fortunes in recent years has meant that fixtures like this will be denied to the hardcore Jack who has served their time at Hartlepool, Doncaster and Orient. The game of the month for Swansea City is Liverpool away, and in true Jack fashion I'm off to Fuerteventura to wash away a very demanding few months both on and off the pitch. This will give me time to write up my scribblings and recall other moments that I have either forgotten, remembered and then forgotten or put to one side due to their lack of significance on me at the time. And anyway, it's freezing cold in the UK and in the mid-20s in Fuerteventura. The beer is cold, the days are long, and the hotel is five-star. With all due respect to Swansea City, it's time to draw a line under the season so far, and quarter off this first 25 per cent with some 5 per cent beers.

The gorgeous Spanish island weather is one thing, the relaxing days by the pool another, but as you guessed it, the day we played Liverpool cost me a fortune. I have a number of contacts at the game, and my travelling companions of Andy Lloyd and Howard Richmond are firmly ensconced in the away end at Anfield. There are many others but my unique ringing tone when they call soon gets them to ring off. That long ringtone as opposed to a UK 'beep beep' certainly puts off the majority of my cohorts.

My iPad fires into life on the free wifi hook-up by the pool, the waiter is bringing me plenty of cold beers and the all-day restaurant is a short stroll away in case the blood sugars go in to overdrive. It's Saturday morning in Fuerteventura, the hotel pool sprinkles a sunny glow across my view and already my sunglasses are melting to my face. I glisten with sweat and the beer quenches any desire to do anything too exhausting. Then I secure commentary links to the game. Could it be any better? I am told by two mouthy and arrogant Scousers that we will easily be cast aside by at least three goals today. I didn't realise how arrogant Liverpool fans are, even when it is clear they are supporting in their minds a team still bragging about success two or three decades ago.

The Liverpool myth of a friendly welcome and a slap on the back was replaced by the truth when forty of us young Swansea fans arrived in the city back in October 1981, as the early morning promise of a football treat gave way to constant attacks on our small but game mob. The slap on the back became a Stanley blade across the shoulder blade and the warm welcome was the trickle of blood across my face. Still, being young, game and full of energy, it wasn't one-way and as the day developed the expected 3,000 Swans fans became 12,000 visiting fans all wanting to be crushed into the away end. Walls collapsed outside the ground as fans were baton-charged by the local police in the complete mêlée that threatened to turn into a full-on riot at any moment. The Stanley Park Stanley blade was returned in kind and in among all this a football match was about to break out too. The 2-minute silence for Bill Shankly in the ground was overshadowed by constant roars and charging from the Swansea support outside. This in turn upset the Liverpool fans who were provoked further. Perhaps the Liverpool fans so keen on recalling past glories would like to cast their minds back to the filthy rows of houses and the urine-stained streets of Anfield in the 1980s. Riots and all.

The trip to Anfield back then was a tricky one to navigate before you returned home safely and hopefully intact. OK, this won't tell you much about the football, but it didn't matter back then, survival was the key. 'Gis a job'? It was 'gis a fight or I'll slice your back', more like. The locals will get no sympathy when the boot goes in outside Anfield, for what you give, you receive – that's the way in these parts. The smiling happy Scouser will welcome you with a boot to the face. Last time I was here for a league game it was a case of fight for your life – for your own little piece of space to stop you being crushed to death or trampled by police horses charging in to a frenzied crowd of away fans. I couldn't get into the away end that day so I paid to go into the home end. When the Swans went one up I and many others cheered and the fists rained down on us in the Kop. Being escorted round the ground we ran a gauntlet of pure hate, the home fans spitting at us. I got in a second time – these people wouldn't put me off. Swansea City fought as hard as our brave followers had to off the pitch. Shankly may well have been recently deceased at this time, but his memory lived on that day. It was total mania as punks, skins, mods and the newly founded soul boys (or football casual) smashed the living shit out of each other. I recall police horses rolling on the ground as hundreds clashed across a dual carriageway after the game, young lads totally fearless in their endeavour to go toe-to-toe in any way they could. Sirens blared out across the community that only a few months before had been engulfed in a cloud of smoke during the riots of '81 in Toxteth and beyond. This was a city used to fighting, used to getting its own way, but today there would be no quarter given. The blood on the streets would run cold as the Liverpool welcome became a football myth – again and again.

This was Liverpool in '82. This was Swansea back then, not a lot of difference, but the same pain. Initially I wanted a day out at the football, but it became for me, a new birth into other football matters. Pure survival became a drug for many and the football culture that was born in me that day stayed for a number of years. As a sixteen-year-old punk rocking skinhead with absolutely no fear whatsoever, be the numbers far too much or the chances of survival not even slim, I didn't care. I was born that day as well as a real Swansea Jack, a participant in the Swansea skinhead army. I had venom in my blood and venom in my ears from the screeching vocals of Swansea City's finest skinhead punks (Skunx).

In those days there was always a Saturday afternoon trouble spot as the firm forged new links and new ideas on the North Bank terraces as the Swans' demise meant other more pressing matters were on our minds. After the highs of Liverpool away in October 1981 and that first season in the sun we never saw the like again.

That is until today. And as that fucking hot Spanish sun burned in to my eyes and the beer was consumed in sunny Fuerteventura I think of all these things and more. My personal journey as a Swansea City (back then Town) supporter may well have started in 1968 on a cold Boxing Day as we went down 5–0 at home to Chester City (yes you always remember your first), right up until that watershed moment at Anfield in 1982 and to today. A complete picture of a Swansea City supporting life. Let's move on.

The football played by Swansea City that fine day in Anfield in 2011 was as good if not better than the football played by Toshack's black and white army so many years ago. A 0–0 scoreline does not tell the whole story as Swansea City dominated the game and afterwards a less-than-intelligent Daniel Agger commented, 'We were running around like headless chickens', while Kenny Dalglish said 'We didn't play well.' It tells me all I need to know about what really happened as we gained another point away from home. Liverpool weren't shit – they were outplayed. The fact they didn't have the ball was because we had it. Another football first spectacular.

If Mark Gower had had a lucky charm in his pocket in front of goal at the end, it would have been a well-deserved Swansea City victory. At the end of the game the Anfield faithful applauded the Swansea City support. What does that mean? I'm afraid the gracious football-loving Scouser does not exist, so why applaud the Swansea support? *Dalglish out!* Well, maybe, but surely not because Swansea City gave you a lesson in football? Your problems run far deeper than that.

Tickets for Manchester United at home are sold out and these games are coming thick and fast. Wow, it really does feel like we have arrived now. The predictions by experts that we would go down is looking a bit doubtful today as Brendan thanks the Liverpool support for their generous applause at the end of Saturday's game. The reserves triumph against WBA at Parc y Scarlets and are on a terrific run in the Premier League South, Leroy once again netting to press his claims for a first-team return. I have a whole page in the matchday programme which also kindly refers to *Swansea City 2010/11: Walking on Sunshine* and gives sales a nice boost. Jon Wilshire at the club has again done me proud and we have a book launch planned in the club shop for the end of the month. It's really looking good sales wise as well, they may even want me to write another! (Which I am doing already, of course). I am called by Michelle in the club shop and she asks if I would mind sharing the book launch with Chris Todd who will be selling copies of his book *More than Football in the Blood*. I can't think of a better chap to be standing alongside. I remember his face when the Swans lost at home to Exeter City in that nearly ill-fated season back in 2003 when he was in the Exeter line-up. He is a true Swansea Jack and a fighter as well. I have just read his book. To recover and fight your way back from chronic myeloid leukaemia says a lot about this guy and it will be a pleasure to meet him.

A very friendly victory for a resurgent Wales side in Cardiff by four goals to one and a beaming Gary Speed also fills me with hope that our new manager has at last seen the light. Speed clearly is in some way incorporating the 'Swansea way' into the Wales mindset at squad level. Of course some of the players will struggle with the concept but stunning performances by Ashley Williams and again by Joe Allen after a late withdrawal by Neil Taylor stamp their credentials all over the Cardiff City pitch, and not for the first time. Coaches take note, the Swansea way is taking off, and triangles are the way forward.

The talk now is all about Manchester United, and this makes me slightly angry, even if I do have a brand new suntan, a rejuvenated outlook on life and a clear view on our assault on Europe. I am still rather unhappy. I am angry that many of our support have not witnessed what I have as our struggle has developed over the years. The new breed of fan will soon disappear if we fall away in years to come. I cannot blame the youngster, you were born when you were born, but the latecomer I can sort of look at in a different way. All clubs have them, it's the way of the football world. Barcelona don't have this problem, because they have never fallen away. Could that be us one day? As I have said, all are welcome, young and old, but I do know a few today who would dearly love to see Swansea City play Manchester United at home in the Premier League. Now here is a football first: Manchester United in eight previous visits to Swansea have failed to win with six defeats and two draws accumulated. They don't seem to like their adventures in the real South Wales. The top of the table still reflects Manchester domination with Newcastle I suppose being the surprise package of the season so far. I don't like Alan Pardew (as a football manager – remember it's not personal, it's a football thing), I don't like his confrontational style when he screams in the face of other mangers like a fool. This is a man representing a football club, and like Dalglish he needs to remember that. If he were representing my business I would sack him for his arrogant behaviour. It's just not called for.

The usual will be wheeled out and the old ties revisited as this clash hovers on the horizon, even BBC Wales cannot ignore the fact that on the day Swansea play Manchester United at home in the league that Cardiff City, their beloved Cardiff City, will be away at Reading.

Cwmdonkin is a cracking name for a community: it has a bowls club, you know, and some seventy-two years ago Kenny Morgans was born and raised there (not in the bowls club as far as I know, but he did play for Swansea Town and Manchester United). He talks about split loyalties for the game ahead at the Liberty. I have to say I disagree with you Kenny, you are Swansea born and Swansea bred, the club that first gave you hope and a football career is the team that you should support today. But of course our own 'King Kenny' does get a lot of guest of honour trips to see Manchester United, so I guess that sways his thinking. Mind you he did room share with Bobby Charlton, the gentleman of the game, and his affinity with the biggest football club in the world shines through. They certainly do look after their ex-players, Kenny even went to the 2008 European Cup final in Moscow when United beat Chelsea. Now that would sway my thinking. Nice one Kenny, a Busby Babe and Munich Air Crash survivor. Alan Tate anyone?

Denis Irwin hails the Swansea style in the papers today. He is now classified as a 'great' in Manchester United terms, so he must be right. Irwin's cautious words ahead of the game tell me that after the excellent result against Liverpool we will greet a United side well-versed in our style and fluency. I am reliably informed by an ex-professional footballer that United will soak up our style in the first 20 minutes before penetrating our midfield and defence to earn an opening goal. After that they will again retreat and let Swansea ask the questions. This will be the game plan I am told. Well, he wasn't far wrong because after a good start the Manchester machine kicked in with a lucky goal after a defensive error by Àngel Rangel, allowing Javier Hernandez to sneak what would eventually be the winning goal. Try as we might as the atmosphere was turned up to full volume, we couldn't get back in the game. Scott Sinclair missed an open goal, an absolute sitter, and Nathan Dyer had Patrice Evra checking his backside for leaks as he ran him down time and time again. After 50 minutes Evra was subbed by Ferguson; having been torn apart again by Dyer he was booked. Clearly Evra was one more tackle away from a sending-off. Dyer killed him. Further efforts by Sinclair again and an excellent Danny Graham strike nearly – oh so nearly – gave us a well-deserved point, but United again, as ever, sneaked a 1–0 win. Phil Jones hit the post but Ferguson sounded well relieved as we headed home and listened in to the radio on the M4. Manchester United weren't classless or clueless, they held out and once again – just like the away game at Arsenal, we were beaten by a quality side by one goal because of a mistake. This is quite a bitter pill to swallow. These points may well come back to haunt us as we go for the title at the end of the season. . . .

The table states we are thirteenth in a league of twenty and Brendan Rodgers talks about a thin squad in his after-match interview, but does not deny his side the plaudits. Alex Ferguson talks more about Phil Jones's defensive play in the second half than his team's attacking style throughout. This says a lot about the game, the way Swansea City played and once again rubber-stamps the 'Swansea way'.

It is interesting because as we put in these excellent performances on the pitch, the desperate media latches onto Brendan Rodgers' alleged 'need to move to a big club to prove himself.' However, on the way home one Howard of Cowbridge mentions this very fact – what if Brendan does move on? Are Alan and Colin being groomed into a sound and comfortable position to stabilise and manoeuvre the squad for a second Premier League campaign? Or if this season does fall away, will we have the same impact on the Championship as we did last time around? Relegation is unthinkable at this time because we are playing so well, but Blackpool (I am constantly reminded) started in the same way as we did last season, and look at what happened to them. If Brendan does leave will Colin Pascoe and Alan Curtis even want the job? I don't think so, not full-time, so I remain hopeful the excellent relationship between board and manager continues for some time yet. Frightening thought though, eh? We can't keep losing good managers and become a fishing ground for Premier League clubs who can't see anything other than an agent's telephone number when they need a replacement player or manager. Can we?

So with more points dropped, and I mean dropped after a magnificent home performance, we have made it to 19 November before experiencing our first home defeat of the season. That ain't bad is it? OK, we are seven places above the bottom, and four points clear of Bolton who are occupying the last relegation slot. This will be a constant watch throughout the season, that third from bottom place. That golden spot four places from bottom will not only secure further millions for the club that finishes there – it will most likely save the manager of that club's job as well.

My time is consumed with my pending book launch with Toddy, getting sufficient books into the shop through the publishers seems to be the hardest thing in the world, but thankfully the club works hard to make it happen. Michelle calls me again to make sure all is well and we have hundreds of books all over the shop. It should be a goer this one! Timing is everything and I honestly think the home game against Aston Villa at the end of a reasonably warm November is ripe for a good old-fashioned book launch. A home game, early kick-off, and queues of willing buyers wanting signed copies is the dream. After some significant sales and a hugely successful campaign with Tesco I am very confident. I get a whole load of good wishes, so many calls that I switch off my phone and the books look splendid next to Toddy's in the corner of a packed club shop. And yes the queues begin, slowly at first as we head towards selling the first hundred in record time. I am impressed.

Then I get a nod from a pretty well-known ex-footballer that all is not well. It's 11.00 a.m., and I switch my phone on. It immediately springs in to life, bleep, bleep, bleep as the text messages stream through. One stands out. It reads: 'Gary Speed has hung himself at home mate, he is dead'.

I am stunned. A Dutch chap asks me to sign his copy of *Walking on Sunshine*. I look at him. 'What mate?'

'You sign, please?' he says. He looks a bit miffed. I sign it and I look at Toddy and then a mate arrives from Gloucester.

'You look like you have seen a ghost,' Toddy says. I tell him the news that Gary Speed is dead and the disbelief I see in his face is repeated as the news spreads like wildfire. The people in the club shop are being told, and disbelief is all around. The queue stops and people stand around staring.

Ex-board member Dai Morgan stops briefly and says there is the possibility the game will be called off. This startles me as well, will they really do that? I'm not sure, and one part of me says they should, while the other thinks they should not. The Welsh players in both the Swansea and Villa sides will not want to play, surely, but then footballers are professionals are they not? I'm not sure how this will all end up, but the death of Gary Speed who seemingly has taken his own life will reverberate through the football world for some time, that's for sure.

I didn't see the TV reaction, what I saw was first-hand reaction from Welsh football fans at the death of the Welsh manager – a man who had so much ahead of him and who had seemingly clicked into place a style of play that was being recognised as a great turnaround in our country's football fortunes. 'Why would he do that?' is echoed time and time again. Financially Gary Speed was a man who in no doubt was very sound and well-off. He must have been so unhappy to have done what he did. People have hanged themselves who didn't mean to do so – did that happen? Or did he just want to end the pain and misery within? Only Gary knows and any searching questions and indeed answers will come on another day, if at all. There will always be a lot of unanswered questions at the end of all this, there has to be – for his family, sons and close friends there may never be closure, we all know that.

The Villa game was a live TV game on Sky. In quick time Kevin Johns admirably coped with the sentiments of us all pre-match and delivered a succinct and sympathetic speech to the Liberty crowd. The stunning news affected us all in different ways, for some it was too much to take, for others a fact of life. I sit in the latter bracket, though sympathetic to those who loved him. At the same time though, very confused as to why anyone would do such a thing when they had so much to give, and so much pain to cause to those who love them dearly.

The game ended 0–0, points shared in a pointless match. The other Sunday game ends 1–1 between Liverpool and Manchester City. The weekend seems empty, even though the Swans have accumulated as many clean sheets all season as Manchester United. We could have won the game easily with Graham, Sinclair and Lita all having decent chances. The failure to score again and end the month without a single goal will not be lost on the media. However, the game fizzled out as expected and the drab draw result was fair. Aston Villa had five bookings and were merciless in the tackle, and for me could have ended up with ten or even nine men at the end. Alex McLeish the Villa manager has his tactics and they don't resemble Swansea's tactics, that's for sure. I rate him as highly as Mick McCarthy at Wolves and Steve Bruce. I put them all in the 'No, thank you' bracket. Not at my club.

The weekend's results see the Swans another point ahead of Bolton who are still third from bottom; we are now five points clear of them and still in thirteenth as the gap widens. Chelsea win, as do Tottenham, and Bolton lose at home to Everton. It all goes rather well for us as a club. Brendan Rodgers will settle down with his hot chocolate tonight safe in the knowledge that we are a third of the way to safety and it isn't even December.

The FA Cup rewards us with a trip to Barnsley in round three. For the first time ever I actually feel we could win it!

Chapter Eight

December: 20,000 Shirts Under the Sea

That's the news story of the week for me, the fact we have sold over 20,000 replica shirts in a few months leading up to Christmas. I can remember when hitting 500 sales in a season was seen as some sort of landmark, but 20,000 shirts is some response from the ever-growing and now-immense Swansea City support. In fact it's the best sales record in Wales for shirts, I will say that again – The Best! We now circulate and sell more merchandise than any other Welsh club, and of course are the best-placed football club with Premier League status in a brand new stadium (well almost) recovering more financial reward for success and generating more fiscal opportunity than any other club in Wales. That is totally amazing.

More amazing is the thick skin of Steve Kean at Blackburn Rovers, who no matter how much shit he has thrown at him remains calm. In front of the cameras he oozes belief and professionalism . . . well, in front of those cameras he knows are recording! The fans are so upset that even the pie sales at the club are down, and season ticket sales can only be described as pathetic. The fans are not revolting in the right way for me though; see the Swansea template and take a chance at running your own club would be my message. They really need to do more than just shout and go home. It's the same at Cardiff City, a club allegedly with Premiership ambitions, but which folds year in, year out, when their mettle is tested. I briefly read their internet forums and see that the majority of messages are statements like 'Someone needs to do something' or 'Who is going to sort this mess out?' Well? How about you? Just an observation on a lower-league club's machinations, but promise these lads and lasses the world and they will gobble it up, that's always been the way in Cardiff. Call them Premier League and before long they believe it.

Sad – very sad. They have been turned over by owner after owner with the gift of the gab. Today they are clearly not the brightest set of fans to cross the great divide. It's almost in sympathy that I say this – they are bordering on the most ridiculous set of supporters to ever be thrust upon the English pyramid system. Turned over, stuffed, mugged and lied to season after season, and what did they do? Nothing, not a thing. They just lap up the next lie. Well, that didn't happen at Swansea did it? And look at us now. Cardiff fans take heed, you're mugs.

Now with that off my chest I look ahead to what I think is a dead cert home win against Blackburn Rovers this weekend. By the way, the Swans are the away team. Yes you heard me right – a dead cert home win. I think they have the beating of us in the strength and desire department, and looking at their recent results and seeing them play they may well give us a bit of a lesson, I reckon. They possess extreme desire for one-off games, but overall, owing to their poor leadership they don't have the longevity to make a season worth the effort. In Yakubu they have a player who would do a fantastic job at Swansea, a total goalscorer and better than what we have at this moment in time. That is not to say that what we have won't improve, but I am talking now, today, Saturday 3 December 2011.

Tickets for the game are flying, and there will be just under 4,000 fans at the game cheering on the team and the players who represent Swansea City FC. Today we play in orange and today I fear the worst, even on the day I am feeling that we should try and lock up the shop and take the Rovers storm head-on before playing a more tactical game. A few people are saying we need a 'Plan B' and we need to show a little more determination in midfield to negate the opposition's tactics. I can't fall out with this, and in Brendan we haven't really seen a man under that much pressure since he joined us. So today will be interesting.

I will say I thought we did this to some extent for the first twenty minutes, and was just about beginning to feel comfortable, especially with our attacking play when it went wrong. Yakubu stepped up and played himself in to put Blackburn 1–0 up, and began to dismantle us mentally and physically. Leroy Lita's splendid finish to a twenty-odd-pass-move was an exception, but overall Blackburn had too much for us in the first half. This was confirmed with Yakubu's second goal – a header on the stroke of half time.

The second half saw us implode and a number of the travelling support got a bit fractious with stewards. I think stewards should steward – I don't know about you? Blackburn's third was another header, and yes, you guessed it, from Yakubu, and even though Luke Moore made the scoreline look a bit more respectable it was never going to work out for us. Then Blackburn scored a fourth, again from Yakubu, and the Jack Army was silenced, albeit for a few minutes. The players get the supporters' applause, but this time I can't do it I am afraid – these are the games that we should be competing far harder to win. I have made my choice, the players didn't give me the effort I required as a fan. Rovers get their first win since they beat Arsenal, and maybe, just maybe, they aren't as bad as everyone believes they are. The Swans lose 4–2, and it could have been much worse.

Scott Sinclair had a good game, and so did Joe Allen before he got sent off for a second bookable offence (ridiculous Mr Moss). We lacked something today, something more than the finesse and panache often associated with our play. Our football gets the plaudits most weeks, but this week it shouldn't, and the learning curve for the manager and players continues. Yes, of course I forgive them; they are young, passionate and want to win. But I can't forgive their lack of effort, and today, it's my belief we lacked effort. We move on having dropped to fourteenth in the league, one place lower than before the game. Around us Norwich get thumped 5–1 at Man City and QPR and WBA draw 1–1. Wigan getting hammered at home 4–1 by the Arsenal is a boost and Bolton's 3–0 loss at Spurs helps as well. The next day Stoke beat Everton to confirm our position and I put this Lancashire hotpot behind me as quick as my memory will allow. Anyway, it's my birthday next week and we play Fulham at home. Three points is what I want, and fuck the gift wrap. Losing makes me unhappy, and no matter what happens next it ruins the bloody weekend. I don't buy any Sunday papers the next day and don't watch any football, that's the way it is. The week will cleanse me – I hope.

A shopping Saturday before Christmas generally means football clubs' attendances fall. Of course at Swansea our home ends sell out every week, and this week with Fulham as the visitors I can guarantee the away end won't. They don't travel well do Fulham, never have, even for London derbies, preferring to fill their own ground and leave their team to chance away from Craven Cottage. This is just the opportunity the Swans need to put last week's result at Blackburn behind them. Michel Vorm says the same, and Joe Allen reflects on his first career sending-off feature on the back pages. Let's be honest, there isn't too much to say after such a disappointing result up north. Fede Bessone voicing his desire to play in the first team caps off a no-news week, and for me it is no news because Neil Taylor and anyone from Tatey (when fit) or even a back three would be preferable to Mr Bessone with all due respect.

I like birthdays for one reason; they reaffirm the fact you are still alive, and that's not a bad thing. Today I want the gift of three points and nothing else. That's the deal.

The first half was a bit dire to be honest, although Leroy Lita looked lively as did Leon Britton buzzing and snapping around the opposition's feet in midfield. Senderos didn't like it at all – he got done time and time again and looked so out of it that he could have been sent off after 30 minutes easily. He wasn't, and how that didn't happen is beyond me when you look at Joe Allen's dismissal last week. Lita has great movement and even though his goals return is poor he made a golden opportunity for himself between Hangeland and Senderos to head wide. Luke Moore who is looking silky smooth today hit the bar with a scorcher, and to be totally honest I am getting frustrated again, purely because we should now be a few up. Scottie had a weak shot saved as well by Fulham's Schwarzer as the Londoners' defence was looking rocky. Up front it is clear why they have only scored four goals away all season; even with the lively Andy Johnson they looked a bit lacklustre.

The second half, though, was a complete change and both sides went hell-for-leather for the win. Now this is what we pay for Jacks, pure passion and commitment. Yes, look at the badge boys, the game is on. Sinclair is busy and a snap shot is deflected to put us one up. Cue complete delirium, and a birthday celebration for me in the Swansea East Stand. All around me the Gloucester, Weston and Bristol Jacks are dancing and celebrating a well-deserved goal. I bet Martin Jol wished he hadn't dropped Zamora now because they need a goal . . . the Swans are all over them. This is Sinclair's first goal from open play this season and he enjoyed it immensely, nearly as much as we did. Kemy Agustien came on for Moore and made an immediate impact, smacking a terrific drive off the bar, though at 1–0 up we still need to hammer home our domination.

Then Fulham started to make a game of it and once again we start to look a bit twitchy in midfield and at the back. Ash misplaces a few passes which Fulham seize upon, and not for the first time this season the usually dependable back four makes errors that are capitalised on by a Premier League attack. Vorm preserved our lead with a few cracking saves and Jazz Richards, who hadn't done that badly on the day, faced up to his tormentor Kerim Frei whom he brought down in the box. It was a penalty and with 4 minutes or so to go it felt like a knife in the heart. But I had a feeling, I get them on my birthday, and sometimes on other days too.

Clint Dempsey didn't look right on his run-up and his shot from the spot was well saved by our Dutch keeper; in fact that's his second save from the spot this season, and a real game-saver. Vorm was man of the match for me and to rub salt into the wound Danny Graham came on for Lita and fired home a second from a Mark Gower cross. Just what the doctor ordered, a 2–0 win and three points in the bag boys, tidy stuff. Swansea dominated shots, possession and for once fouls with only Vorm getting yellow carded. Surprisingly, despite Fulham's strong-arm tactics, they only got one booking, and that's the only draw they get all day. Jol in his after-match interview talks about deserving to win or maybe draw. The man is mad and looks it too. If I were Bobby Zamora I would check my pillow for a horse's head tonight. Brendan smoothly addresses his interviewer with the usual well-mannered responses and well thought-out recollection of the game as it happened. He represents the club so well in front of the camera. Today I feel this is in complete contrast to one Kenny Dalglish who is arrogant, rude and stubborn. Does the man not realise that the American owners of Liverpool won't like their brand being represented in that way to the worldwide media? Is he that stupid? The same can be said for many people in football; they are too blinkered to see when they are being found out, too uncaring to know when they are bringing themselves, their club and the game in to disrepute. I wouldn't want my business being represented on the TV in the way that Dalglish represents Liverpool – it's nothing short of a disgrace and for him to think it's OK utterly amazes me.

It was good that we beat Fulham though, as Norwich stuffed Newcastle 4–2 and Wigan won at WBA. At the top end Arsenal won again 1–0 and Manchester United hammered Wolves 4–1 at Old Trafford. The big game of the weekend saw Chelsea beat Manchester City 2–1 at Stamford Bridge. It's hot this Christmas, and Citeh's defeat at Chelsea narrows the gap at the top, but they stay there, two points clear of United. I immediately look ahead to Newcastle away next week, the Saturday before the Christmas madness and fixture overload.

The contacts I have in football I hold extremely dear, and some are good friends who have my utmost confidence. I am hearing today, a cold and grey Tuesday in mid-December that an ex-Reading player is being sought out by Brendan and he is keen to get him in to the squad. At this time I don't know if it will be a signing or loan signing, but either way a few more calls reveal that Gylfi Sigurdsson is the target. He is an ex-Reading player at 1899 Hoffenheim in Germany, and very much out of favour with current boss Holger Stanislawski, a manager who after just a few months at the club is very much out of favour himself. Hoffenheim have had three managers in about a year or so, and the club seems to be in a bit of turmoil. I remember Gylfi at Reading. He always gave us a hard time and I didn't realise he was so young – only 22. He's one of those players who seems to have been around for much longer. If we get him in I reckon he will improve us immensely and is as good or in most cases much better than we already have.

Newcastle away is a hell of a trip and I will put my hands up and say I don't like the place. The Big Market; the short-skirted, drunken ladies bobbing about all over the place, spilling forth their wobbly bits; the accent; the nightlife; the bars and restaurants and the laugh. Nah, not for me, I'll stay at home and nurse my injuries! Yeah right. The game at Newcastle doesn't hold the same fears of a recent trip to the north-east when we got a bit of a spanking. I reckon we can get something here and even though the game itself saw us under the cosh and maybe a tad lucky to get the point, as ever in football you get what you get. And we got a valuable point. Alan Pardew made the mistake of trying to stop the Swans playing, as opposed to hitting home the clear advantage he had in his playing staff. Well, that was mistake number one. The second was not pushing forward their advantage as the game went on and the Geordies put us under pressure. The Swans' eight clean sheets clearly worried him and they panicked when we ventured forwards with Wayne Routledge cutting inside the opposition's defence on a number of occasions in the second half. Shola Ameobi was thwarted by Vorm who was again in fine form – he had to be as Newcastle sought the win. Pardew's second mistake was taking Obertan off (although he may have had a knock) and then Tiote, which also surprised me and a number of Newcastle's more vociferous fans. We had a charmed life at times but we also had chances to win through Sinclair and Routledge, and overall we deserved the point.

They say things come in threes and Alan Pardew's third mistake of the day had to be those frilly pink knickers he wore under his suit. Nah, I'm joking he only made two mistakes, the third wasn't a mistake at all. Ask any Southampton fan.

The youth team have had a remarkable run as the season has progressed and players coming through like Jandir Zola, James Loveridge and Scott Tancock to name but a few are really shining as the young starlets ripped Liverpool apart at the Liberty, a game I happily watched on LFC TV for free and have to say the commentary was particularly biased, ill-informed and persistently unprofessional. Apart from that it was magnificent. The pass-and-move tactical style and intelligent football started by Roberto Martinez and Graham Jones is now free-flowing through the first-team squad, reserve sides and youth teams. My good mate Ian Williams watches the youngsters a lot as his partner's lad, Dan Eddolls, is a keeper in the junior set-up and he agrees that the Swansea City way is present throughout all our teams. Fantastic. Keep an eye on Dan as well, he was proudly pictured in *Walking on Sunshine*, and from what I am hearing (and not only around Swansea) he is one to watch in the future. He may need an agent very soon!

The fantastic draw against Newcastle, and the spirit we show gives us all renewed hope that these very tough games away from the Liberty won't be as hard as we thought. The footballing sides in the league, like Newcastle and the top six teams, seem to suit us better than the tough and uncompromising sides scrapping away for a morsel of hope at the bottom. And the next trip just a few days after the draw in the north-east takes us to the north-west for a night game against Everton. The old ground that is Goodison Park was another lowlight of previous journeys north for me personally. The welcome at Goodison in the dark and distant 1980s wasn't that warm. The area around the ground was torn to shreds and a burning pit of fire and hopelessness back in 1981 as the country descended into social unrest. The Thatcher years had drawn a line dividing south from north and this was reflected in Wales as well. Long before the miners were put to the sword by a government that couldn't bear the union stance or the left-wing militancy of Wales and the north, areas like Liverpool were already burning pure hatred.

Thirty years later Goodison has changed, although the stands are still the same. Decrepit and tight seating, falling away in places, and beneath them a terrace that reminds me of a hundred years of hope and lost faith, not dissimilar to the old Vetch Field. The hot food outlets spill out a disgusting mix of fatty burgers and chips for £3. The game is all-ticket, £30 on top of petrol, food and an afternoon off work to see a night game at one of the oldest grounds in the world. I can see it now. If I close my eyes. The seating so tight it hurts. The welcome so insignificant it hurts. The journey so uncomfortable it hurts. The hurt so fucking hurting it hurts. The jolly reporters, the ex-players and so-called football people who summarise, talk and pontificate don't know about this type of football pain, nor do they know of any history that comes with it. The real football fan knows all-too-damned-well how it feels to scrape together the money to pay in at the gate, while the freeloading Charlies look down on them like they're sewer rats.

Goodison has an eternal flame of hope, the fans more genuine and more intelligent than most. The so-called second club in a proper second-rate city spills forth an attitude I like, and one that I trust. The 'knowledgeable' Scousers in red bear no resemblance to the blue hordes of Goodison. The game itself was awful, and the Swans under a floodlit glow of hope looked like they may well grab another well-earned point. The luck we had at Newcastle deserted us on the hour as Leon Osman scored an emphatic winner which was greeted with a high-pitched Scouse scream more than a roar, a very odd noise for so many to make at the same time. It almost put me off the aura of the place. Louis Saha missed a sitter as did Drenthe, then Johnny Hetinga and Coleman did the same. The Swans were rocking and only Danny Graham came close to restoring some hope. We had four shots on goal all night, and we lost our industry, guile and purpose. We seemed tired again. The midfield was in need of an injection of something, but it never happened. Under the Goodison floodlights my fears returned as they did after Blackburn away. The midfield needs something more than Mark Gower's tireless running and exquisite passing style, and yes I mean that. He may well feel he has made the grade in the Premier League, and I agree if only he could have that extra piece of football skill in his armoury. Maybe the boy Gylfi from Iceland will restore some faith, but we need that now, not in two weeks' time. The Merseyside air is cold, the feeling in my toes has gone, and we return to our abodes a little lost and a little less confident. For all the hope in the world I will never get this day back, and for that I feel quite sorry.

But to hell with it, Christmas is round the corner, I feel well, the diabetes is still there but controlled, it could be a lot worse, eh? Last year I had swine 'flu and wandered the city of Gloucester in my fucking sandals dragging a Christmas tree behind me like a tramp in drag. So, yes, things are much better this year.

Even after the Everton defeat we are fourteenth; we seem to like it in fourteenth, and all of us I am sure are happy with the way things are panning out. I am in a local boozer with a few mates and one from the other side (my good mate Clarkeson the Cardiff fan – his name's Nigel, but Claaaaaarkeson sounds so much better in his silly dialect). At the bar in my new Swansea City top I encounter a fellow Jack who turns to me and says, 'Hey, who are we my friend?' as he slaps my back and tells me all about the Swans. I am intrigued so test him out.

'So, do you think Vorm is as good as Rog?' I've been here before and I know I shouldn't do it. I welcome new fans as much as any fan should, but I am drunk and feeling fidgety.

'Rog, yeah . . . old Rog – great manager.' he responds.

'I meant Rog.' I said 'You know – the bloke we signed from Chelsea, "back in the day" as those darn youngsters say.'

'Yeah, mate,' he says and then turns his back to me. I laugh, then smile, tap him on the back and say 'It don't matter mate – no matter who we are or where we are, we are Jacks remember.'

I invited him over to our small posse of Swans fans and Clarkeson, the unlucky one. He looked uncertain. He smiled as well though. Then left. I haven't seen him since. It's the way of the Premier League, I suppose. There is no point in pretending. There are one or two I have encountered over the years who if they were before me now, the end result would be devastating. And my long memory never forgets, and to that end that devastation is still to come. Did you really think I had forgotten, oh no, not me – tick, tick, tick . . . bang.

It's coming.

My thought processes are not as they should be (is it the time of year that does this to me?). The stress and pressure of the festivities, the family and the lash make me succumb to darker thoughts, miserable endings and pointless retribution. Or maybe worthwhile retribution? Probably, and I feed off this emotion well. I am hopeful too that our Swans players this Christmas can swallow their turkey and do the same. Get angry and then get even, no matter how long it takes, if possible do it in the 90 minutes, not twelve years later when they least expect it. Let's get out of this mess. I feel relegated, down and out. I have gone all Ian Holloway – all negatively positive – as Christmas comes and goes with a home draw against QPR. A bit of a bogey club, these Rs. Their fans are arrogant and they have an intolerance of all things outside the capital city. Four brave QPR fans saw the light outside the ground. I said to one, 'Mate, keep it down. It's funny, I know, shouting "sheepshaggers" continuously, in fact you're hilariously funny, but not everyone will laugh.' He didn't listen and unfortunately for them not everyone laughed, and their night was ruined.

This attitude sums up for me the QPR fan, a horrible specimen moulded out of hatred and jealousy that they are sixth-rate. A club so ruined by their unsuccessful past that it surfaces in their twisted faces, twisted opinions and twisted minds. Are they all like this on a matchday? I hear they are, but surely not? I watch a documentary about previous owners, and see an attitude not dissimilar to that of the fans who frequent their stands. They deserve each other. QPR: absolutely pathetic, ridiculous supporters.

The big games are the ones we all like, no matter how long we have supported a club, for these games loom on the horizon like a glowing beacon. The object on our horizon is a New Year's Eve kick-off with Tottenham Hotspur. Harry, the good old barrow boy – cheeky and chirpy, slightly flighty and a 'man of the people'. His car-crashed face from the 1960s tells a rugged tale of football domination in recent years, his blinking analysis and openness is a media whore's dream. The press love 'our Harry', the nailed-on candidate for the England job, that international team of no-hopers who cheated the Germans in 1966 and who in turn reaped their Teutonic vengeance from the penalty spot for years to come. The international team that everyone thinks is the best but is the worst because it fails, cries, lies and cheats. That England. Geoff Hurst off the bar; Harry Redknapp off to the bar; Jimmy Greaves, where's the bar? Yeah, they know how to live, these boys. If the years of stress don't get old 'Arry, the tax man will, but he has a lovely dog, and a Rosie 47 bank account that will appear at Southwark Crown Court very soon. Credit to the man, he really seems to think he is going to walk free from all the bother he is in, and carry on and dance his way in to the England job after Tottenham are compensated from that big pot of money that people like Harry take for granted exists. I'm out of a job, the phone rings, I get what I want. I dip my hand in and take what I want, and care not for the consequences. Me, me, me. Oh yes, dear managers and players, you don't have a job, you 'play' for your money. Not like most of us. No early start for you – just a gentle three-hour day and millions to boot.

Now Harry Redknapp comes across as an honest chap, so I surmise from this (I speak as I find) that he must be. His dog barks, the bank manager jumps and all of a sudden we are dealing in offshore revenues. Everybody is allowed to I am sure, I don't know too much about it, and Harry must remain not guilty, unless of course he is proven otherwise by twelve good people of decent character.

His Spurs side is a credit to the club. They are bloody exciting, very dominant in most games and have Gareth Bale of Wales in the set-up. A monkey-faced man of indiscriminate values on the pitch – sorry but it's true. Gareth has an extraordinary ability to dive and cheat as well as be 'nearly' the best player in the world. I mean that, honestly. He has all those assets and I want a picture of him eating a banana just to convince myself he is a monkey. I suppose he is in the Peter Crouch bracket. What would he be if he were not a professional footballer? In Peter's own words, 'A virgin.'

The pubs in Swansea are crammed to the rafters and the atmosphere is smoky (but smoking is banned so fuck knows what's going on there). It's one of those cold evenings that you get in the winter which comes with that welcoming and not unpleasant smell of chimney smoke. The vendors are vending and the walls of the public houses are bending. There is some hatred here as well some slight taste of confrontation. This makes it that much more interesting, that old Vetch spirit mustn't leave us entirely. During games like this we need a lot of noise. The walk in the fading light from pub to ground sees mainly Jacks mingling and singing, the drinking on the last night of another year already taking effect. You are allowed to drink heavily at rugby, shout, swear and discriminate. But at football? Oh no, there is an Act, it talks of offences, and often offends. It is liberally applied at times in contravention of common sense let alone an Act of Parliament. In Maesteg as the peanut flies over the posts, the beer flows freely, and that Welsh passion is allowed. In a place called 'Liberty' in Swansea, there is none. No liberty, no common sense and no equality. We talk of equal times, but in football there is none, never was, never will be, regardless of the location.

Harry is in fear I reckon. Howard agrees and Kev who met us with a hop, skip and a jump similarly concurs. We could be placing the heads of these cockney wideboys on spikes before the end of the day. Rafael van der Vaart is a player I like a lot. Like Van der Valk he detects things and like that old-style Dutch detective he appears and strikes when you least expect it. He hunts his quarry well, and is a Premier League nightmare when he wants a little taste of the action. Assou-Ekotto needs some explanation as well, what a head of hair that man has! An almost clown-like barnet of extreme wonderment. He is rubbish though, I am told. I'm not sure – let's see if he has a new hole ripped out of his rear come the end of the day. 'Dobbie's in mush!' I hear mentioned. 'Dobbie – yeah! Dobbie's in, Dobbie, Dobbie, Dobbie!' The name reverberates around me as the teams are announced.

Andy boy says 'Fuck.' I again remain silent, unusual I know, but this is his chance, the man's opportunity to stake a claim, make a statement and thrust himself into to forefront of Brendan's thinking.

Mark Gower starts, an ex-Tottenham player that nobody really remembers in North London I am told – which is a bit sad – and Jazz gets a nod as well with Rangel on the bench. Monkey boy plays as well (what?! No, dear reader . . . I am not talking about Bale). I'm on about Garry Monk, captain fantastic, the ginger gymnastic. The Caulker can't play today: loan agreements and rules only made up by those with little else to do as Steve sits this out, and silently hopes we win. Danny is on the bench again and is looking to enter the new year a little more confident and a little bit more in the forefront of the manager's mind for first eleven selection.

Garry Monk has that song in his head I reckon, 'Stuck in the middle with you', as he looks to his left and right as the game commences. With Friedel busy and Vorm a spectator, the Swans are looking good again; this could the scalp we predicted at the start of this season. We have shots cleared frantically away by a dodgy-looking Spurs defence not well marshalled at all by Kaboul and Modric. Gallas has a touch of the Williams and Sinclair is on his game at last. Scotty is showing himself to be the quality act that he is, which during some games he has failed to come up with this season. The Monk man looks solid and Taylor as ever, a reliable and well-rounded defender making little or no fuss as he slides passes around the pitch from deep. Ledley King is missing, and to be honest I would have loved to have seen him up against this vibrant Swans side. I think his lack of anything I see as talent would have been blown apart by us today. Some players have a charmed life, and I reckon Ledley falls in to this bracket, a non-training professional footballer who like Paul McGrath at Manchester United years ago glided through it all unaffected by the whole scenario.

For Spurs to win this game they would have to breach the tightest defence in British football today, this is fact, and even though we have only won one game in nine there is a complete belief that today will see us well-rewarded for our efforts. The crowd is crazy, loud and dominant in the song stakes, while the London boys are quiet, bemused and pretty insignificant. As expected.

Jazz gets ripped a bit by Bale as he is taught a lesson time and time again, the ball being propelled from one side of the pitch to the other. Bale dives, and gets booked for cheating – as stated before, this is what he does. Often. Joe Allen makes a rare mistake as the Dutch detective hammers home a cracking opener to put Spurs 1–0 up. A cracking effort indeed. It wasn't deserved but once again a Premier League hotshot hits home a body blow to Wales' premier football team. This calls for character, guts and even more determination.

Now, Dobbie. No impact. Where is the fast-moving, quick-thinking elfin figure from last season? Is this a step up too far for the Scotsman? Can he not reproduce the influential style that secured his place in Swansea City history? Well, no. He looked laboured, slow and out of sorts. This must have been noticed by Brendan Rodgers and Colin Pascoe but little if any change is made. The Dobster does have shot which is blocked by Kyle Walker but little else goes for him. I feel sorry for him – he wants it, but he isn't good enough today. Is he good enough for the Premier League?

Then Rangel broke free and delivered a decent cross which the Spurs defence seemed to want no part of. They were just not interested in any type of clearance and were found wanting. Ekotto sliced it, the keeper seemed to be nowhere and sub Danny Graham did enough to allow Scotty-boy to pull the Swans level. It was no more than we deserved. The goal was greeted with an enormous wave of noise as fans fell over each other to celebrate a fantastic move and goal. After that the Swans could have won it, probing to snatch all three points. Post-match Harry was as honest as he could be in his assessment that they got lucky on the day. Brendan was equally as media-savvy as he again intelligently analysed the game and added his key words like 'group' and 'philosophy' to an ever-increasing dialogue which the media are currently lapping up.

The journey home was jolly. We all agreed it was the end of a fantastic year, a year that nobody could have predicted twelve months before. How the hell are we ever going to match that? is our constant thought. The turn of 2011 saw us hopeful of the play-offs, and then when we reached them we were just hopeful that if we were not to make it then the same fate should be Cardiff's as well. Winning on that dramatic day, and the emotion of that Wembley triumph has since moved to fears that the media are right and the writing professionals have it spot on. The year progressed, the nonsense prevailed, the squad was announced and the fixtures drooled over. It's the end of 2011 and we are in fourteenth in the Premier League. Five points above the last relegation spot is an achievement that very few outside of the Jack Army predicted. Football has won the day – the midfield has dominated and Leon has sparkled, Danny has hit form and Scotty is on fire. Nathan is as agile as ever and Routledge adds the fear factor when he has a go as well. At the back we are solid and Taylor, Williams and Rangel are tight and in sync with each other. Monk comes in and carries that captain's arm band so well, Joe, Mark and Kemy have added to the strong and dominant midfield too. With a few additions this premier journey may well be one we can handle, build upon and push forwards. I am bright, confident and happy tonight. I open the door of my house, the family are there, my grandson runs up to me and laughs throwing his arms around me. The whole thing, this life, this journey, is presenting me with so many happy moments that you really wouldn't want it to end.

The Swansea City journey makes you cry, laugh and breathe pure life in to what for many of us is a mundane and only tolerable existence. Money, family and friends all add to the mix, a happy mix of comfort, wonderful times and total bliss.

Tonight I am a few days in to my forty-ninth year, and today, this New Year's Eve, I am so fucking happy I could cry.

Happy New Year.

Chapter Nine

January: For those of You about to Rock, Nathan Salutes You

S o this is our first New Year in the Premier League, the first Welsh football club to reach this league and our first visit, every away game, to the grounds that now host Premier League football. That is, as a Premier League side. We have been here before as the *last* Welsh club to play at this level, the highest level in the football pyramid in the most-watched, richest, most popular league in the world. My word, how bloody green-eyed those losers down the road must be. If I could insert a smiley here, I would.

Our first trip away this year will be Aston Villa and Howard is in the know as to where to go, where to park, eat and drink. But we stick with the majority and later on in the day probably repent at our leisure in streams of traffic. For the WBA away trip things will be different. I also know that the loan signing of Gylfi Sigurdsson has gone through, late on New Year's Day. The ice man cometh. The midfield dynamo, striker of superb free kicks and midfield battler is a Jack until May. Welcome my son.

Gylfi's current club, Hoffenheim in Germany, don't seem too good at PR, a bit like Kenny at Anfield – the tirade of words are often challenging, confrontational and not exactly conducive to good business. They really don't like it up 'em. They seem negative to Gylfi's move as to the player's ability at their club. It won't stop them asking for £6m or more if he comes to Swansea, though.

As the Arsenal home tickets are announced they quickly sell out and the Jack Army take a full complement of songsters to the

Birmingham area for a game at Aston Villa. We park for a fiver close to the ground and search out the recommended away pub. Locating that was easy, and in the cold we stood having paid some £2 for entry into a fucking shithole bar, cold and unwelcoming – a bit Hoffenheim in its attitude – and security staff that are used to pushing people about. Well, my previous experience tells me that this sort of behaviour will only be tolerated for a while before something gives. And it does. And that's the way the cookie crumbles. Slightly dilapidated housing, glancing eyes and fast-food outlets serving some damned good food litter these closed-in streets. The beer was rubbish though, but to be here at this New Year gathering was a pleasure. The Villa Park I remember when I last came here when we shipped five goals quite easily hasn't changed at all outside. I assume they have seats inside, close together, uncomfortable and restricting. Of course they will. The toilets I can imagine also, few in quantity, full of sweating bodies and the odd plume of blue smoke rising in to the air as the punter pisses. It's a scenario we have all seen many times as a fat steward tries to locate the offender, not that this happens at rugby.

It is cold. I see a few kind faces and friends and then see one that isn't and just smile – time is on my side with him – he quickly looks away, cowardice evident in his eyes, looking for solace in his few mates, people who know exactly what is going on, and want nothing to do with it. He knows, deep down, he really does. The away entrance is navigated. Then I get a text from Mick from Weston: 'Orlandi is playing, I'm going home'. I am surprised I have to say, but I think, as I have already said, that Orlandi has the match for the Premier League. I think his skills base will be well suited to this challenge, and if he has added a bit of strength to his game he may well surprise us all. Nobody is convinced this is a good move and many murmurs about 'starting with ten men' are made. The starting eleven is different to the one against Spurs and QPR. This doesn't surprise me either after the manager's grumbling about playing too many fixtures over Christmas. Now we have been here before, and Brendan doesn't often annoy me, but this does. This warm and cosy football life is hard work, eh?

Orlandi, Agustien and Routledge all start and the support is not exactly buzzing with excitement at the thought of these changes, but I in fact trust and agree with these decisions. Villa are on a poor run, they have a clueless manager, and a very angry support that doesn't want Alex McLeish anywhere near the club. The ex-Birmingham boss appointed in the summer has had a rough ride since crossing the Birmingham divide, and I can't see it changing. We just need to do a Wolves on this team, add a few goals to the mix and we could be celebrating our first away win of the season. Ah, another football first. The support is noisy, happy, drunk, pointy and confrontational – all more than matching what Villa can chuck at us from the very start. From above, in the stands around us, the Swans' support is so noisy, so challenging, that the Villa support can only watch and listen to a booming 'Hymns and Arias'. It's electric. You can see etched on the home fans' faces that they cannot match this Swansea City tirade of noise, they cannot even try. The famous Holte End is silent, quiet and looks weak and abject. They are a support going through the season's motions with their almost motionless team.

From the off we are at them, biting hard into the tackle and searching out width via Nathan and Wayne. Britton's probing passes are ripping Villa to pieces and it took only four minutes for the brilliant Nathan Dyer to send a shot flying past Guzan in the Villa goal for 1–0. The supporters went mental, Nathan ran towards the noise which was almost grabbing him in to the crowd as they surged forwards. He stops, he smiles and salutes the Jack Army thousands. Game on Villa, now where are ya? They weren't anywhere, and to be perfectly honest I was disappointed that we went in only one up at half time – it should have been four. I suppose this is the reason why I felt uncomfortable at half time, queueing for a brief urinal break among the predicted blue smoke, pushy stewards and beer-breathing Jacks. The consensus in the bog was that we should have this match slotted away already. I knew it would only take one goal to get us rocking again, and hoped that it would be early and come our way.

Thankfully it did and it was Wayne Routledge who got it, scoring his first goal for Swansea City and indeed, his first Premier League goal after playing for about five hundred clubs in just six years. He looked so happy he ran and twisted in his celebration, not knowing where to go or look, and the game for me was won even before the Villa second-half tactics could kick in. Their support turned on McLeish who had the usual 'Sacked in the morning; taunt from the Swansea support. Villa are a set-piece side; they lump the ball forwards with little style and much hope, and the Swansea defence, marshalled by Ashley Williams, soaked up the repetitive strain football from the beleaguered home side. It was easy. Yes, they had a few chances, but the Swans and Danny Graham in particular had at least five, and by the end of the game with the Swansea bar rattled just once, the game was indeed won. Villa are a hopeless case and their fear of relegation is certainly real.

The introduction of Sinclair and Allen for Orlandi and Dyer inserted some more flair into the midfield and Villa looked a broken side at the end. Orlandi had played well, probing and passing in midfield, and taking a shot on from some twenty-five yards that threatened to go in before veering to the keeper's right. It was as complete a performance as we could have wished for, slightly like the Bristol City demolition last season at Ashton Gate. Villa were crushed. Our football nous and style again secured the points. It has to be said that this game wouldn't have been one the 'experts' would have expected us to win, but we did. Put that in the points tally column Brendan, the Jacks are back.

Elevated to eleventh in the league we are now looking upwards and not downwards, but at the bottom there is an eight-point gap between us and relegation. I am beginning to believe again. Did I ever say that I didn't? Of course, I can change my emotions with the click of a finger, that's the way it is following Swansea City. Click, switch, click, change – BANG! Fucking fuse blew. The New Year is still happy.

We don't have a home game for twelve days which eases the club into January very smoothly. I think long and hard about the cup tie ahead at Barnlsey. We old-timers of Swansea past have been here before, and the thought doesn't thrill me, so I send a correspondent instead, one Howard of Cowbridge fills my ears with news of the resplendent Swans who eased so majestically passed a pedestrian Barnlsey side. Oh how we have improved in the past twelve months. The ease of the 4–2 away victory inspired by Dyer and Rangel in the main was a pleasure to watch on a special receiver in a location we couldn't disclose in case I am found out! Oh, of course this is now allowed thanks to the Portsmouth pub landlady who took on the authorities – nice one. The small person strikes a blow for the rest of us. The small people of Swansea City do the same; Britton and Dyer indeed are giants against this type of meagre opposition. It's so easy. Winning cups does not bother me, neither does anything other than Premier League status come May 2012. That is all that matters, and beating Barnstonforth in the FA Cup means absolutely nothing, indeed again winning the FA Cup means absolutely nothing if we are relegated as well, ask the Birmingham supporters. If your absolute goal is getting promoted or staying in a league and you get to a cup final and the knock-on effect is relegation, what's the point?

All eyes are on the next fixture, Arsenal at home, and I am hopeful that Wenger, their one-eyed manager, sees and conducts himself appropriately. I hope he doesn't moan and drag his own negative issues into South Wales with him. The Arsenal side are staying overnight in Swansea and I am alerted to a whole load of people outside the team hotel as the Arsenal players, including Thierry Henry, walk along the hotel front pre-game. They are followed by a plethora of people who I can only describe as an absolute embarrassment to the city of Swansea. I understand also that this footage appeared on YouTube too, so I check it out, and sure enough yes, what an absolute embarrassment. They are shouting players' names and following them around like puppies. I am told about this occurrence by a member of the Arsenal staff. He stated that the way these ten or so people took photos and scuttled about after them was so embarrassing that they went back inside. OK, if you're an Arsenal fan that is fine, but some were so-called Swansea supporters, so can you not conduct yourself with a modicum of dignity? These are the fans who many dislike, and you know exactly who you are. Absolutely tragic people.

This, though, is our centenary year, and even if I can't get along with everyone, many people have many, many memories about their Swansea-supporting past. A website is set up to collect as many of these memories as possible and I am proud to be asked to contribute in some small way. Recent events see the signings of Situ confirmed and the race for high-flyer Rory Donnelly from Cliftonville is also won; brilliant work from the club in overcoming Liverpool and Everton for the signing. I don't see any of these players featuring this season, however they certainly will do in the future if their press is to be believed. In Donnelly's case it is nailed-on. He should be a Premier League success, so work hard my son, get your head down, listen to your mentors and I guarantee with finishing like you're capable of we will certainly see glory for you. He needs some strengthening, that's for sure and if he applied himself in the right way the future is so, so bright for Rory.

Moras has left the club, and this doesn't surprise me at all, he has hardly featured and the end of his three-month contract sees the end of his Swansea City career. Brief, moderate and forgetful.

The centenary of our club has seen the cabbage patch become the Vetch Field and then the Liberty, right through to the Swans becoming the Jacks. It's been such an uplifting ride. The sad and dark days of the 1980s and the early part of this new century were hard to work through, but we made it as a club. This is what makes us all so special as Swansea City supporters, so very special it makes your heart skip a beat, and swell with pride. The supporters have saved this club – it is here purely because of the efforts of the few back in those dark days when all *certain* people wanted was to hammer us in to the ground and steal all they could. Those evil bastards aren't so clever now are they? 1912–2012 is one hell of an achievement.

None of us around now can know what it was like to be a Swans fan back at the start of it all, but this is slowly being documented and put together in fine style by a keen group of fans. From the first song to burst out from those carelessly assembled terraces in 1913 to the 'Swansea oh Swansea' ballad, it is clear we are very proud people. In fact this first acknowledged song is so intriguing that I will publish it here:

Look out, here comes a crowd of jolly fellows all looking gay
Bent on a visit to the football field to watch two teams play
Which side they favour you will quickly know, when both lots
   turn out,
For when 'Nick' or Hamilton lead their boys upon the field
You'll hear them loudly shout —

Chorus
We are the Swans' supporters, we are the village boys,
When our team is playing, hear us all hurrahing,
Shouting, Coleman, now then, SHOOT for goal, man,
Now, Bally, pass it to Swarby, Jimmy don't, shoot too far;

It's in . . . (ha! ha!) we grin (ha! ha!)
We make an awful din
As we all shout hurrah!
If we should travel by excursion when our boys play away,
Our antics create much diversion, for you'll hear people say
Who are those noisy lot of bounders who command all the train?
The word goes round that they don't know who we are,
Then we all sing this refrain . . .

Chorus

What an incredible song from a fantastic and interesting time!
I can't imagine it echoing around the East Stand at Swansea, it is
most certainly of its time, but examination of the lyrics sees a similar
attitude of expectancy and hope, including camaraderie for a Jack
Army very much in its early formation. The world then was on the
brink of the First World War and these Swans supporters know
this as well. This song displays the battling qualities of those old
Swansea Town people. The true spirit of old, fantastic passion we
all know so much about and which some of us have witnessed first-
hand. The song talks about travelling away by train, those faces and
hopes – all dead now – once carried the Swansea spirit to other parts
of the country. Noisily and proudly too, and what a wonderful time
that must have been, on the brink of a world about to self-destruct
they still find a Saturday outing to be the best moments of their lives.

Maybe these dramatic chants from the Swansea fans then helped
the side to triumph as they did, winning the Welsh league and Welsh
cup nearly a hundred years ago? Unbelievable stuff.

Huw Bowen's wonderful examination of the 1920s and a Swans
player named Jack Fowler is so cleverly written and exposes his
passion for the club as well. Fowler was the first Swansea hero,
the first Lee Trundle, Robbie James or Alan Curtis. A man who set
records in a side that also contained Billy Hole and when the Swans
support came from across the whole of Wales, Ireland and the
north of England. I suggest you check out the piece written by Huw
on the Swansea centenary website. It's a wonderful compilation
of memories and facts from eighty years ago. The Swans were a
national force back then and made it to an FA Cup semi-final too.

Today as I and my weirdly assembled friends gather in Gloucester for the trip back to Swansea, we can also take time to think about our own Swansea memories. Today though is just that, it's about today – a day when Swansea City take on Arsenal in the Premier League on TV at the Liberty Stadium. A moment of history in the making for Swans fans in years to come to cherish. Those smiling faces and happy Swansea folk will be captured too, just like those faces from the 1920s, no different in their hopes and aspirations when the Swans take the field. No different at all. We are so lucky.

The money that flows through the fingers of football people is a dream to many normal folk, and the supporters of the Swans now know this. We now have supporters who talk in millions with no perception of a million pounds or multiples of that amount. We need a £10m striker is becoming a regular statement from the teenage fanclub of Swansea now. This young, special but naïve new supporter sees the Swans flash across the world of Sky TV and takes it for granted. This is good, but also comes with a warning from us older and wiser supporters. Can it last? And if it does are you ready to step forward you young Swansea fans of now and fight? Fight to the bitter end?

To win today the team have to earn their crust, that is a stone-cold certainty. This Arsenal side goes from greatness to has-beens a week at a time. This is the key to our potential success today. Place these Arsenal players under extreme pressure, get in their faces, play our football and keep it Swansea. Easier said than done I am sure and the game displays a real desire, at last, a desire we have all called for on a number of occasions this season already. It's the desire that was missing at Blackburn and Everton and it is very evident today. The weather has had a bit of an impact on the pitch which although patchy from the peanut-chasers running about on it a few days before, doesn't stop our free-flowing game. What a magnificent performance this turned out to be.

Robin van Persie's opener for Arsenal just fired the emotions even more; a well-taken finish it was, but the reaction could not have been better. Scott Sinclair riddled and wriggled them with skilful moments of pure pleasure and Leon Britton jinxed and tricked his way through the Arsenal midfield. Swansea were pushing these North London giants to the limit. The Arsenal back four was miserable and out of touch as Dyer, Allen and Rangel ran at them.

Forward into battle we cried and forward they went – straight for the throat. Sinclair converted a penalty after Ramsey fouled a busy Dyer and the first half fluctuated and surged with all our emotions. That smell, that acrid smoky smell, returns to the cold January air and the light fades as the flying Swans push home their authority. How the half ended in a draw is difficult to fathom, but it did and the second half surely could not be as entertaining? Of course it was, and it was littered with goals as well. First it is Swansea who after a magnificently cool move go 2–1 ahead through Nathan Dyer. A move mastered in Narberth by Joe Allen robbing the idle and complaining Ramsey of the ball and his dignity for Dyer to fire home. Now we are 2–1 up, and the stadium is rocking so much I fear it could fall down. Yes, Arsenal did try to make amends, as did Ramsey, but Ash and Caulker remained firm and Neil Taylor was again splendid. Wenger started his arm-waving, remonstrating about God knows what, his actions bringing jeers and cries of laughter from the stands as he shouted. He is now the master of his own undoing. Does he not see this? The more he shouted and complained, the madder he got, and in turn the worse his team played. Now crouched down and contemplating his next complaint, the Swans nearly go 3–1 up. Staying at 2–1 won't win the game, we go to sleep momentarily, and Arsenal squeeze an equaliser through Walcott, inspired by Henry. The silence was deafening and the travelling Arsenal support cheered as much in relief as celebration. We looked bedraggled as Brendan issued one last war cry from the restart, clapping his hands, as did the rest of the bench. The Swansea roar came from the pits of our stomachs at the restart.

Straight away we move forwards through Rangel and then sub Gylfi Sigurdsson and within seconds of Arsenal equalising Danny Graham fires a shot hard and low across Szczesny in the Arsenal goal. He dives and the ball fizzes in to the back of the net. Goal! The Swans are 3–2 up, and this time we cannot contain ourselves. The surge forwards and the jumping and cheering Jacks are in dreamland. The mighty Arsenal are down and out, knocked to the floor by pure football skill, they have no answer to this goal. More chances came our way and one from Arsenal's Rosicky from long range saw a nervy ending for us all, but at the final whistle referee Oliver, after 5 minutes' added time, drew matters to a close. Where did that extra time come from? It's easy to speculate.

After-match plaudits from across a bewildered but appreciative nation flood in, even Talksport radio for once conceded some ground. The British football world is witnessing a new way of playing a complete football system, moulded by a professional outlook and group mentality that many clubs can only dream about. On *Match of the Day*, Lee Dixon tries to explain it in a word: *triangle*. He demonstrated Swansea's play and magnifies the approach to passing and moving. He is in awe of the progressive style and the magnetic genius of the players involved. Analysing matters from back to front the winning goal is featured, explained, reviewed and drooled over. Surely Danny Graham's best and most favourite goal to date has pushed Swansea City in to the minds of many football fans tonight. A 3–2 win sees the Swans fly upwards again, and tonight we are tenth in the league with twenty-six points, only four wins away in my estimation from safety. QPR are third from bottom on seventeen points. The gap widens and some Swans fans talk of Europe – no fair play entry though, but a straight entry through league position. Of course this is utter nonsense, it won't happen, not this time around, that is surely an impossible dream. One blemish on the day's events is the whining Arsène Wenger – not happy to concede defeat admirably, he bemoans the Liberty pitch. He harnesses his own agenda and spews forth a miserable epitaph to a joyous Swansea day. Why could he not just be, for once, concessionary in his interview that on the day they lost the game to a better side? Like Harry Redknapp, why could he not just admit that, for once, his overpaid stars did not match the football guile of a superior side. It was of course too much to ask as the pitch is blamed, the referee is blamed and I am sure the young bloke on his first day at Rossi's chippy would be blamed as well if he could.

Josh McEachran now joins from Chelsea on loan, and many can't see why this young man with so many plaudits is joining an already magnificent midfield at Swansea. I think about this for a while and see the benefits for this young man. It isn't just about 90 minutes on the football field. At Swansea he will gain some serious experience in our free-flowing football style, be a part of a group of players who are bonded and focussed, and he will also be mentored in areas of the game we don't see as fans on a matchday. He will learn all about team spirit and organisation and as a part of the squad (playing or on the bench) he will no doubt gain assurance in his own ability as well. This is all about learning. He will see a maturity in our play and develop an educated style that will see him return to Chelsea at the end of the season a better player, squad member, and most importantly, in fact far more important for me, a better person. This is why Josh is with us now, and in Brendan and his staff there is no better place for him to be to learn a little bit more about his football trade.

At Swansea we could easily sign brilliant players who for 90 minutes could bring some degree of glory to our club, but clever Brendan knows it's about much more than that. The dressing room needs to be a tight unit with little disruption. This area of the club needs the Tommy Butlers of this world to maintain an equilibrium and the Garry Monks to be the go-between from manager to player. This is a careful plan and one which all successful football teams have. Unless of course like Chelsea you have big egos who care not about who they affect, as long as they get their own way. They put themselves first, not the club. I mean, who wants that at a football club, not me, that's for sure. Josh will learn this as well and very quickly pick up on this senseless attitude when he returns to Stamford Bridge. Education is paramount for us all, we all learn in different ways and this Swansea experience will be a participatory one for him over the coming months. A psychomotor experience. The best and most effective way to learn as a young person making your way in the world.

The scrap at the top of the league is between the red and the blue of Manchester with Spurs in third. Chelsea beat our next opponents, Sunderland, in London, but not convincingly, and the Mackems should have won the game. Norwich get some acknowledgement for a 2–1 win at WBA, but according to their moaning supporters, not enough, and the Stokies snatch a point at Liverpool. Wolves gain a bit of ground as well drawing at Tottenham 1–1. It all looks pretty good for Swansea City in mid-January. On the Monday of a busy weekend Manchester City beat Wigan who are now in a desperate position at the foot of the table on fifteen points. City stay proudly on top of the best, biggest and most-watched league in the football world by the fact they have scored more goals than their bitter rivals. This is a league that includes Swansea City. Our team.

It is the Swansea way as well that we celebrate a wonderful win with a slump. That is what we do as a club. The fans are raised up high by those chosen few who do our bidding on the pitch, then returned to the abyss a few days later. A mere six days later in fact, at a cold and blustery Stadium of Light, the Swans were battered back in to their boxes and firmly punched out by the Mackems. The debut for Josh is insignificant and he looks weak in possession and loses his will and fight very quickly. The forward-dominated Sunderland side pulled us this way and that as we missed chances at one end and they made us pay at the other. Sinclair's miss followed by a wonder goal from Stéphane Sessègnon, a sublime effort so fast-paced and curling that Vorm had no chance. This came after a period of domination that should have seen the Swans in front. This Martin O'Neill-led side crushed home their advantage which was mainly in the pace and passion department. Hustling the young Swans off the ball and cruising forwards, always looking dangerous. They were in charge and never really under threat as our charge up the league was brought to a halt by a second goal from Craig Gardner. I suppose up until then we had glimmers of hope and opportunities to snatch what would have been an unworthy draw. These things happen in barren landscapes and cold biting places like the north-east of England. These things are expected. O'Neill's men had been just that – men. They are on a wonderful run of results since the sad and hopeless Steve Bruce left the club. He has inspired so much the spirit that this side needed to stay in the Premier League. The journey home, and clearly our Danny Graham doesn't like all the travelling, will give the players time to ponder and reflect on a job not very well done. The 64 per cent possession stat is pleasing, but on this performance all it does is fuel those blinkered hacks and fans of other teams that Swansea City can retain the ball but do little else with it. The Arsenal result is gone, and all we have to remember now is this last outing. A week is a long time for anyone, in sport, work or indeed, waiting for a bus.

The ups and downs continue and Lee Lucas, one of the brighter young Swans, is off to Burton on loan, and they seem very pleased to have secured him. We do need another success story like Joe Allen to justify the investments made in youth football in Wales. As the biggest club side in the Principality we need to progress this side of the business as the next few years come around.

Although I still believe in the FA Cup as a supporter of our country's football, a run in this competition is now exactly not what

I or anyone else connected to the club really want. It will take our eye off the ball, that much is true, and after the last result I think this has been reinforced. Bolton Wanderers away is a game that will quickly pass me by as we all look to the end of the month and Chelsea at home. In fact our cup exit at the hands of an inspired Bolton side didn't affect or bother me that much at all. I was far more displeased with our exit in the League Cup to Shrewsbury than the loss at Bolton.

The FA Cup tie team picked by the manager displays my thoughts on paper and on the pitch. Gerhard Tremmel in goal while Fede Bessone, Jazz, McEachran, Leroy and Moore all start and put up a decent if not convincing display. Luke Moore had forged us ahead, and to many it was undeserved, but the way Bolton equalised, well in to first half injury time, was again disappointing. The scorer, one Darren Pratley, netted having hardly had a kick in the first 45 minutes. The much-changed Swans did rally in the second half, and hitting the post became a regular event again before Gerhard's fumble and Chris Eagles' winner in front of a quiet support and a respectable and noisy Swansea following was enough to see our dreams, if indeed we had any dreams of FA Cup glory this season, in tatters. Just over 11,000 fans at the Reebok tells us all how interested the majority are in this tie. The team fall again in one of the tougher games in one of the tougher areas of the country.

However, fear not all ye brave men and women of Swansea present. For this week we have the blue side of London visiting us. Not the hypocrisy that is QPR, no, our visitors will be singing 'Blue is the colour, football is the game'. The football club that produced Osgood, Hutchinson, Webb, Harris, Houseman and yes – Hollins – is coming to town on a midweek night that will no doubt increase the fantasy of the occasion under floodlights. The media are interested and John Hollins slowly (very slowly) talks in his very best Hollins whine about what he thinks will happen. I can't take him seriously at all. The man that I remember drawing in pictures at the age of seven for a school project, may have been a hero on the field in the 1970s, but he was never one off it as far as I am concerned. His links and history that saw the start of this great club's demise in West Wales is unforgivable. Totally unforgivable.

Huw Jenkins reflects on more determined times to save our club this week and I read with interest his views on how it all came about. It is of course no different to mine, and maybe yours. That raw feeling clearly still remains for him as it does for me. He chooses his words far more carefully than I need to, or will do, but what he says about how the coming together of us all is all that I and many need to read. He understands all too well how he is, where he is today, and how our club is with him too. It is apt and right that his reflections on that hard work ten years ago coincides with the visit of Chelsea FC rubber-stamping the success the club have had after many years of turmoil and hard graft. Let's not forget as well the very many sacrifices made both professionally and personally for us all.

The season so far has been so magnificent and pleasing that why should I now look back when I can look forwards to such a wonderful Premier League tie featuring my beloved Swans? Nothing should take away nights like these and nobody will be stopping me from getting to this one.

A calendar month from that successful result at home to Spurs and the home win against Arsenal now supports our belief that Chelsea can go the same way too. On a night that will see raw emotion bleed from those stands at the Liberty and pure passion seep from its very guts, I feel we have hope in abundance. It's cold, fucking cold as the wind hits my face when we leave for the walk from pub to ground. The voices are so excited and anticipating a bloody encounter with the English from across the bridge is on.

> The walk, the stroll our happy souls
> They head straight down to see
> The wonderful and exciting play
> That comes with this city
>
> No journey less for any life
> Should ignore the way they play
> The fight, the guts and all we see
> Down here in Swansea Bay
>
> And when the roar it greets you all
> The team they rise and score
> The excitement is on every face
> The Swans they win once more

So for all you people everywhere
Come see the Swansea play
The white shirts of this new-found love
Is Premier in every way.

These words are crashing into my mind as we walk fast, walk tight, breathing the Swansea night air as the light from the stadium comes in to view. We have been here before, the Swansea history is around us, sounding out our trust in faith and once again clashing with today's new history.

'They will talk about nights like these in years to come,' I say to Howard.

'Just like we talk about those nights back when we were kids.' he replies.

We are tight, we are right, we are Swansea. This modern-day event cannot be matched by anything. No Olympic torch or two-week event can capture any fan's imagination like these precious nights and times. It's so raw and now it is at the back of everyone's throat. There are twisting runs across the road, dodging cars; everyone wants to be there now, at the ground, not stuck in traffic. For the mere catch-up of a few seconds lives will be put at risk as darting figures, far too impatient to wait for a green pedestrian light, dash from here to there. A man falls and is hit; the car screeches and he gets up. This seems to be a fixture – at these fixtures. Madness ensues, metal and skin collide, and a spare ticket is available. The trot and run, the lights the sights, this is Swansea.

The ground is bouncing, pointing angrily toward an assembled army of blue. The East Stand bawls their fashionable hatred of Chelsea. The big time Charlies, the small time hooligans, the headhunted minority mostly old and dead are the focus. The noise is hitting record levels. The Stokies would be proud of this rabble, and the tie is off and away as the ball hits the lights, shining and gleaming under the watchful eye of referee Andre Marriner. A full-house watches a packed Chelsea defence plead for mercy as the Swans hit full throttle from the off. The relentless Chelsea challenges overlooked by the referee (maybe he likes to see a challenge) but then picked up on when returned by an indignant Swansea team make the crowd even more hostile. Five bookable offences are ignored as Nathan is brought to the floor time and time again, and when

Neil Taylor does it once he is rewarded with a yellow card. It makes the night that more hate-fuelled. The referee doesn't realise that his mismanagement of the game is actually working in our favour. The step up in play and noise as Sigurdsson starts pulling the strings is tangible; it has its own force and the free kick he delivered which merely set up an exquisite Sinclair finish puts the Swans one up. He answers all his critics in one second of brilliance. This is no depleted Chelsea side with Torres, Mata, Sturridge and Meireles all pushing forwards and supported by Ivanovic, Luiz and Cole they search for an equaliser. Cole at last gets his card and is walking a tightrope, as do Malouda and Meireles. At last the referee remembers that blue is *not* the colour, and I can see that now he stays away from the touchlines, not utilising all the pitch as most refs do. Does he sense the twelfth man wants blood tonight? Cech gets plenty of goalkeeping practice and the night runs its course with a second half that entertained and tore at everyone's heart strings. Essien hit a hopeful shot goalwards and Bosingwa probed at Rangel's parts as Chelsea searched for some saving grace. Nathan missed a chance to seal matters and the fourth official signalled 6 minutes of injury time. It has its place, and tonight the mismanagement spreads far and wide making sure Chelsea get all the opportunities they can. An appalling decision, and to cap events Marriner has at last grown a pair and sent Ashley Cole off, a clumsy defender not worthy of any plaudit, only among the glossy magazines with a woman who deserves it even less. Chelsea are down to ten men; Swansea are defending too deep and the inevitable happened in questionable added time . . . a deflection from Bosingwa's half-shot struck Taylor and spun in to the net. The Chelsea fans celebrated a draw at little Swansea, as did their expensively assembled team. Swansea were dejected purely due to the fact that they deserved the win. Away from the pitch both managers look happy, and the man they call AVB, head of the Chelsea dynasty (for now) seems almost jubilant. If he were to lose here tonight he would be gone, down and out.

The result once again makes the football world draw breath. Swansea City dominated a Chelsea side searching for success in the FA Cup, Champions League and Premier league. A team so expensive it shines ignorant, self-indulgent football madness in dollars and pounds. Those real Chelsea stars of years gone by will be (mostly) spinning in their graves. It's a ridiculous price tag for a ridiculous ensemble of players who stink of everything that I hate in football. Their greedy demands should have been punched and kicked to the ground at the Liberty tonight, but a failing football management system from the officials, and a terrible decision-making process put in to effect by the referee made the whole night conspire against us. The super Swans earn a point? No, Chelsea earned the point, we had a win taken from us by a desperate conspiring need to support the big boys.

I sound like Arsène Wenger, do I not? I know I do. And I know I should. The journey home is reflective, Kev knows, Howard knows, Andy knows that this was a game we should have won, but we are still so proud tonight. The journey again throws up more talking points than a daft-sounding Collymore could beg for. His pleading for people to phone in to his sorry show gets some sympathy from me. He is a lost soul. Some of us only have one hope, I fortunately have many and many things to live for, and occupy my time. In Stan I sense a man desperate to be loved, desperate to be understood and most certainly desperate for recognition. When he had those opportunities presented to him as a younger man, he spurned them. I suspect today he regrets that very much indeed.

The month ends and although we are now not in the FA Cup and I don't care. The thirty-one days of this month have been pivotal. We have negotiated Arsenal and Chelsea and have taken four points from them, four points which will no doubt prove very precious come May. The away demolition of Aston Villa was the most pleasing game for me – it was a great match for any fan to see their team win. We are 'walking on sunshine' in the depths of winter, and we shine like a golden star in a grey and hostile sky.

We are Swansea. We are winning.

Chapter Ten

February:
The Iceman Cometh

The bitter cold of a winter's morning greets the skin, and all areas south of the top of my head are already as numb as a Columbian's nasal passage. The Gloucester skyline is grey, and the foreboding is just that – foreboding. It's nine o'clock in the morning and my mobile sparks in to life. Dave Naylor is on the other end predicting doom and gloom for the day, and not in a football sense either. The Baggies of West Brom are ahead of me and various others in this sleeting and biting weather. It's just fucking miserable. Dave has been chronicled many times over the years, in books, in text messages and many other forms, and usually it's about the weather. He is the Swans' all-time director of weather forecasting. A man of many hats, but today, no matter how woolly your hat is, you're going to feel it. 'Wrap up,' he says. 'Aye, OK Dave'; 'Watch the roads,' 'Aye, OK Dave'; 'Take a fluorescent jacket and shovel mate,' 'Aye, OK Dave.' I now question my commitment to the day's game. I fear that we are in for the weather apocalypse today. Howard of Cowbridge arrives, not happy. He has got snow on the brain. Andy from Gloucester is here – well, he looks a bit happy. And the rest of the Gloucester Jacks are going straight to the ground. We are an odd presence, all of us together on a Gloucester housing estate, as supporters of a Premier League club, when all through our supporting lives the smiles and smirks from other football fans, often behind our backs, was as evident to us as they were to those that dealt them. The status as a laughing stock of football, the taunts and shame, the misery and blame has long gone. These days it's plaudits and pats on the back, handshakes when we win, as if it was us who played the game. People see Swansea City on *Match of the Day*, believing the hype and not understanding the past, the cold fear of obscurity now clouded over in golden glory. Dire is no longer a term to describe us, but the name Dyer is on the tip of everyone's tongue. How much times have changed and over such a small timeframe.

Of course we are going to The Hawthorns. For me trips away are like pints of beer. You are each given an amount of beer to drink in your life, once its gone, its gone. You can drink it all at once or savour it over a period of time. Either way you have an exact allocation and that's your lot. This principle can be applied to many things, if not every thing. Your allocation of away trips following the Swans can also be applied to this. So it is essential that these days away following the Swans are enjoyed and held dear. Howard states that local knowledge is precious, and we really should listen to him more when he talks about the West Midlands, once the natural haunt of this once Bromsgrove based jack. Having discarded his knowledge for the Villa away game in a bin in Handsworth and ended up in an extra hour's worth of traffic, I see much value in taking on board his efforts to avail us of his wisdom for this game.

I have been to West Brom many times, won a few, lost a lot, and every time the queue of traffic (and the parking) and pubs have not been good. Howard is our local guide today. He takes us off at junction 2 of the M5 and it is a decent start as predictions are for a Swans win. I am not so certain, I feel much the same as I did for the Chelsea game, uncertain and unsure. Having seen the Sunderland game disappear in a cloud of north-east mist and rain, it's sometimes hard to predict which Swansea team will turn up. Much the same as Everton away already, and Norwich. This is a hard one. How cold can it get today? And how cold is it now? The wind is biting as we park up at Langley Green railway station, a free spot for the weary Honda to rest while we find this oasis of a pub in the middle of an urban wasteland. Boarded-up houses, businesses long gone and industrial reminders of a more prosperous time are all around us, as the snow starts to fall, and our hopes of finding any solace today drop dramatically.

Coming off the M5 at junction 2 didn't feel right. Howard was confident though, and very assured that what we are doing is not only right, it's the only thing to do. Parking at WBA is horrendous, getting away from the ground is even worse and it can take ages. Our parking slot looked good, albeit the car was quickly covered in snow, the pub was just around the corner – warm and welcoming – and even the chavvy locals didn't seem bothered. Maybe Howard has come up trumps? A quick perusal of the menu in the bar proved right and from that moment onwards I was filled with a warm glow, not of expectation for the game, but for the people present and the journey we had been on. Phil Sumbler turns up with his daughter and Mick Cannon, Tom, Rich and his kids along with Howard, Andy and I. We are all there for one cause. Swansea City.

So I recommend the Crosswells Inn to you all for any West Bromwich trip. They served up one of the best chicken baltis with half and half I have had for many a year and the Guinness was gleaming. I am not a pub guide for football fans, but this place requires a visit. Could I have been anywhere near a perfect football day? Of course, though I am a Swansea City supporter, and anything could happen.

What happened was this.

My telephone rings. I go outside into the sleeting blizzard; it's my wife who was en route to Cheltenham for a day out with my two daughters. The car she was in has had a blow out, it spun off the M5, crashed into a barrier and is almost certainly a write-off. Everyone is OK (but she would say that). I press her further, knowing that she doesn't want to make a meal of this event. I then get out of her that my youngest daughter (well, she is twenty-four) has gone to hospital, purely for a check-up as she is pregnant. That doesn't fill me with happiness I can tell you. I press her further and further until I am sure that all is well – the car is dead, that's fine – but when your whole life is contained in a tin can and it crashes in the way it did, let me tell you, football does not matter, and all you want to be is there with them to make sure they are safe. They are all going home, the day cancelled, and all is well. It checks my mood, and makes me angry, it also makes me think. As I walk into the pub a chav-type pushes past me. No apology. 'I do apologise for getting in your way mate,' I say. Honestly, how quickly can one person's mood change. I make a snowball and aim it straight at the back of his head – 'Nice one mate,' he laughs. I quickly start to relax and my tension subsides, I forget that a lot of people are selfish fools. Many don't share or care. He walks away shouting, 'Hope you win today, fuck the Baggies.' The jostling, pushing and arrogant culture of this country takes one more step backwards.

And it's a fine line which we tread as to which side of it we stand on. Aggression wins.

Although the family are safe and all is well I think about going back down the M5. Within 10 minutes I assure myself that all is well and football wins, well, it would do wouldn't it! A happy family at home equals a warm glow, a happy football team is just that, and that emotion changes quickly.

The short trip in by train from Langley Green to The Hawthorns is a recommended one, a couple of quid on a return ticket should assure us of a quick getaway after the match and in this weather that's a winner for me. Crammed into the carriages are Swans fans and home fans, no hint of bother, and this is what football should be like. All aboard the football express! Howard is onto a winner here. But the snow continues to fall, and if anyone had any doubt that winter isn't here yet, today signals it most certainly is. The trains run still, no leaves on the lines but they are cold lines to negotiate this afternoon. We have never really had that much luck at The Hawthorns (as I have said), we have had some joyous times on a few occasions, but we haven't really melted them here properly. Today, we could do that easily. Roy Hodgson is an experienced manager – not my cup of tea – but he does equip his sides with belief and strengthens them at the back. If we get our way down the flanks today they may need it.

I can't shut up about the snow – it was awful. I really did have concerns about the game being called off. On arrival at the ground the Swans support – sold out and packed tightly into the corners – was loud, and in some places very drunk. The cheering and jeering as the Baggies shouted obscenities from both sides was accepted gratefully . . . and then returned in equal measure. The fast-food outlets in the away end are poor, the toilets are disastrous (blue smoke, stewards, etc.), but they will be opening up the turnstile gates for a smoke at half time I am advised.

The game isn't as slippy and slidy as I anticipated. The pitch is well kept and the layers of snow add to the feel of the Saturday afternoon. Siggy is now pulling the strings brilliantly in midfield and is world-class in his thought and play. He's a majestic signing who now, according to most, must be secured permanently by the manager. Our orange shirts and yellow ball are set against a Hawthorns backdrop where the Baggies' old-fashioned stripes clash with a grey, overcast sky. My feet are freezing, and the hopping from foot to foot only makes it subside momentarily. We dodged no bullets today, and even though the home side went up the field briefly and scored through Marc-Antoine Fortune, a two-goal salvo in a matter of a minute and a bit clinched the points. They were deserved as well; this was a side who had not won at home since November. The home fans were not happy – they quickly berated everyone including themselves as the Swans passing game took hold. Siggy, yes magnificent, Danny Graham finding space and time to score number ten of the season completed what turned out to be a stroll in the park. The forays forward hitting at the heart of the West Brom defence saw them capitulate as the game drew to an end and an inevitable win for the Swans. Throughout the team we had given a complete performance, the passing game winning, and goals to boot. We could be happy with whatever weather hit us on our way home tonight. *Match of the Day* saw us catch of the day as once again the pundits drool over our standard of play and Brendan once again conducts an interview with class and very poignantly explains the day. They now have Gylfi to talk about – a man as cool as ice – and wonder how Swansea had found and introduced yet another player to the nation's TV screens that the majority had no idea about. Alan Hansen likes him and talks about managers not having the ability to know about players such as this. I like him as well, and agree for once with Hansen. He doesn't have the answer as to why managers can't find players in the way that Swansea do, though.

Tenth is now the new fourteenth, and the Swans are firmly there on thirty points at the start of February – maybe eight points or so away from safety? I think this may be the figure, other opinions range from forty-four (madness) to thirty-two (I wish). Our magnificent result against Arsenal is once again put into context as they beat Blackburn 7–1 while Wolves, also visiting the capital, snatch a win at Loftus Road. Manchester City beat Fulham 3–0 and a watchable 3–3 between the Chelsea and the best-supported team in West London – Manchester United – draws the weekend to a happy conclusion. City are now two points clear at the top from United; Spurs and Chelsea occupy the next two spots with Newcastle in the surprise slot of fifth. Arsenal and Liverpool are closer to Swansea in the points stakes than the title. Above us are Norwich our next battle royal at home and the most impressive side for me at the moment, Sunderland. A 1–0 win for them at Stoke as hard-fought a victory as you are likely to get in the Premier League.

As predicted, Brendan Rodgers picks up the Barclays Premier League manager of the month award for the incredible spell the side has had in January. The football world will once again take good notice of this feat, and the sides reaching for success at the top of the Premier League will also note his progress. When I see a replaceable Ferguson at Old Trafford, an AVB in turmoil at Chelsea and a completely incompetent Dalglish at Liverpool, I feel very happy we have him with us, at the moment.

The body-blows that are being felt at the foot of the table by Bolton, Wigan and all are not in any way a worry at the Liberty. In no way are we covering up and protecting our stock down Swansea way. On Saturday we welcome last year's fellow promotion rivals Norwich to the fortress. And their fans who have been moaning continuously about Swansea being recognised for their football, and Norwich not, will be there as well. On the pitch they are different. I see a hardened side with Grant Holt at the fore, a strong and progressive attacker who should be an England player. He scores goals, as does Danny Graham – another who may be deserving of a pop at sporting the three lions (even if they have not been too successful of late). They both maybe could change their country's international football fortunes. I only say this because every tournament and game England play they seem to be favourites, and now I hear journos talk of the forthcoming Euros. England are not in the mix, no longer are they world-beaters and dominators. I know why they're doing this – before, when 1966 was in memory (and for forty fucking years afterwards), the journalists have always stated England will win, so if they keep saying they won't – they might. Which makes them even more ridiculous than usual.

The game started so well for Swansea, Danny Graham sticking his foot in and playing the first cards to put the Swans one up early on. It was a coolly taken goal, and he should have had more as the domination of the home side took hold. Except for the inclusion of McEachran it was a pretty strong side that took the field, I felt, for Josh once again really doesn't look like he currently has the strength for the game. That doesn't mean to say this very young man won't have that strength in the future, but that won't serve us well at all today as he is robbed and closed down as the game progresses. Gylfi is almost missing, only playing bit parts and Dyer is not in any way his normal self. We need some refreshing. Having said that there isn't much else to choose from in the squad stakes, and if there is any cause for slight concern it is the club's strength in depth, but then I suppose if you don't have much 'in depth' then the majority of players are happy. That breeds complacency though, and this surfaces as this game moves on.

Norwich hit the bar and they hassle and chase down everything, their desire is far more than ours and we acquiesce quickly, folding in to ourselves Sunderland away style, Norwich away style and Bolton in the cup away style. You have to admire the frequency of those Norwich attacks, they seem as pissed off with us as their squalid and pointless supporters. This is most disconcerting, and to reinforce this we have absolutely no idea what to do. The ball started straying and Ash stopped playing, his assured style left in the dressing room as was Neil Taylor's usual ability on the ball. Norwich closed down our back four, and forced us back, panicking our flowing style to such an extent that we collapsed. Paul Lambert had got it right, Brendan Rodgers had got it wrong, and that manager of the month award seeks revenge very quickly. The gong that causes more losses and crosses than any other award wins again. And that is all that wins. We are left with more questions than answers today. Norwich don't steal the game –they win it hands down. Grant Holt scores two and Anthony Pilkington snatched the other. The defence is the reason in my very humble opinion . . . it collapsed out of sight. Perhaps it's a decaying formula malnourished through overuse, and too much getting its own way. The players at times are maybe too used to making mistakes and not always getting punished. Well today, it was flattened. Even Graham's twelfth goal of the season from the spot didn't cause much cheer, and right at the end had Routledge managed to score (unlikely), a draw would not have been deserved. Happy now Norwich fans? You got the plaudits. Now fuck off.

I have at last entered the world of the twits. On Twitter Joey Barton seems to magnificently manipulate other people's words (which he has read or been given) – using prose to gain votes is in order for the convicted lunatic, I suppose. OK, well let's see how this goes then. I see the football websites and forums, I peruse them rarely, and don't really see much personal value in them. If you have an opinion it is quickly done down. They are abusive and threatening at times, so I find it a pointless journey and one that I won't be on at any time soon. On Twitter the collection of friends or 'followers' seems to be the in thing and I see people begging for them. I think I will just float about and have a look for a while.

The fact we lost at home to the Canaries is one thing, but let's be honest, can you ever imagine losing at home 5–1 to your closest rivals? Well, that's exactly what Wolves have done and this spells the end of their manager Mick McCarthy. The humiliation of a home defeat in this way should signal the end for any manager, especially one who has had such a long and charmed life as he. 'I am a blunt man,' he says, 'I am straight to the point . . . I am what you see and I am what you get'. OK, that's enough. It is obvious why he got the sack.

Elsewhere the Geordies get beaten 5–0 at Spurs and the old-style rivalry of Manchester United and Liverpool sparks in to life and United win. And let's draw a breath for a minute or so. Luis Suarez participated in a racist incident in October 2011 involving Patrice Evra, in as much as he used words which in this country are considered racist, and are not tolerated in dialogue as they create a clear cultural insult. He never seemed to realise this, neither did Kenny Dalglish, nor anyone with the use of the Liverpool brain cell at Anfield. In fact old-timer Dalglish allowed his players to wear t-shirts in support of Suarez, and continued to berate and confront anyone who tried to manage a conversation with him about his opinions and reasons for supporting Suarez. After Suarez was disciplined and admitted using certain comments towards Patrice Evra, Dalglish continued to acknowledge the disgusting nature of this incident and continued unchecked by the FA, Premier League and – I will go further – the law of this land. Dalglish misguidedly went on supporting Suarez, supporting racism and allowing it to flourish within the ranks of the game. Time and time again he had the opportunity to reinforce the issue to a worldwide media, but he chose not to. This moronic attitude was also unchecked within the hallowed corridors of Anfield and all I heard was, 'He is a legend'; well, for me, it matters not who you are. His approach and strategy (if he knows of the word) were flawed, offensive and at best ill-advised. Kenny Dalglish is perhaps not the brightest spark.

His screwed-up face and glaringly ridiculous responses to questions display a man deeply entrenched in his own press, and believing of it in the extreme. He represents the club on *Match of the Day*, Sky and any number of radio stations, and the point here is he represents a brand – that brand is Liverpool FC, one of the biggest brands in world football. The US owners of the club are fully versed in branding, perception, public relations and what the media can do for a club. In Kenny's case the media need do nothing, at times there is no need to draw out the issue, those right-thinking people in sport and elsewhere will know exactly how he is being perceived. And so will the Liverpool owners.

My final point on this disgusting incident and the foolish behaviour of Suarez today when he again refused to neutralise the situation and shake Evra's hand is this: Dalglish is a dead man walking, and he's a ticking time bomb entrenched in the 1980s who will be booted straight out of Anfield as soon as the season ends. Would you want this type of person on every media feed representing your business? Would you be allowed to talk and respond like this by your employers if you had the opportunity to display a professional front to their business? They would throw you to the dogs. You wouldn't stand a chance – you, my friend, would be unemployed. I stand by that today in mid-February 2012 I will leave this piece to fester here and see if I am right at the end of this season. I don't think I will be wrong – Kenny is in the last chance saloon and he has nobody but himself to blame. The quicker people like Dalglish are run out of the game, and there are many, the better it will be.

There is much glee in the club today as Brendan also pens a three-and-a-half-year contract which supporters greet with cheer. I still feel sad for those who idolise people like Brendan and the players at all clubs, that goes without saying, but I too am very pleased. He is the exact opposite to Dalglish; a club man who is fully aware of his responsibility and professional conduct in front of the camera. He would never behave in any way other than that which is appropriate and professional if he were faced with such a situation. A good coach he may well be, a good strategist he most certainly is, but what makes him appealing most of all is his ability to front a football club in the face of questions that are maybe searching, difficult and confrontational. He's a true professional, a man in the zone and aware of the learning curve he is on as a part of his managerial apprenticeship. Always learning, always searching, always aware. He will appeal to many, and to secure him now is a very wise move by Swansea City FC.

Included in the contract is a release clause which will bring in £5m if Brendan were to move on up to a higher club and better brand. Again a wise move that I think would have been more appreciated in the boardroom than in Brendan's comfortable Swansea abode. However, he does cleverly reference this clause in the pre-break press conference and associates it with 'leaving the club in good health' should he go. This I feel is at the back of all our minds, but the fact it is now there in a contract is well . . . interesting and very, very timely.

There is a weekend off ahead, which not only gives me some time away from this damned keyboard it also gives the players time to relax in Tenerife. I notice that the media are already searching for stories as immediately the football power lines are down and news is at a premium. I have no fears for the players' behaviour in the Spanish sunshine, and Twitter is alive with excited players going away and looking forward to a relaxing few days away from Premier League pressure. So as the squad head south to La Caleta for sun and non-alcoholic drinks, I head to the pub for some winter cheer. It's horrible out.

My eye is firmly on the Britannia for the following Sunday as we take on Stoke City in one of those games which will certainly test our ability to travel and take on the physically demanding tactical sides. This will be one of the toughest tests away from home we will face all season, and I include the big names here. Stoke have a hostile crowd, it works in their favour. The ball in the air is a tactic, but it's not their only tactic, and many more discerning football watchers know this only too well. A Sunday kick-off owing to Stoke's successful Europa League campaign does nothing to encourage fans to travel to this one and I get the feeling on the day that we will do very well to get anything at all apart from admiring glances at the teams' new suntans.

With Fulham and Wolves picking up away points and WBA hammering Sunderland (who since my love-in with them have not won much at all), a point would be just what the doctor ordered for me today. I'm not feeling too well; a few chest pains make me

draw breath but apart from that it's onwards and upwards. This
season's tests are not at Old Trafford and Stamford Bridge; the real
examinations will be at places like Stoke, Bolton, Wigan and Fulham.
Hardened sides used to the cut-throat Premier League. The big shock
as the supporters get to the ground is no Michel Vorm in the starting
eleven, rumoured to be injured. Gerhard Tremmel gets the nod again,
and in a way I am pleased as he has the opportunity to make amends
after his ordeal in the cup at Bolton. I just hope he doesn't get it all
wrong again this time when points mean far more than prizes.

Possession is key again, and to describe our passing game as
slick is an understatement as we start well and take a hold of the
game. Scott put one over the bar, and Nathan worried the wings as
the game evened out. Stoke hit us hard at set pieces and Tremmel
had to be on his mettle early on to keep them out. He does look a
tad nervous though. Upson rises upwards as a cross meets his nut,
leaving Gerhard scrambling in mid-air, and Stoke go one up. We try
to hit back but the Stoke players, many of whom missed Thursday's
Europa game to concentrate on today's game look fresh. We really
don't look anything other than tired. Peter Crouch was next as a
high ball again was headed goalwards and Tremmel should have
done far better, fumbling the ball over the line; now it's 2–0 and all
hope is pretty much dashed.

Stoke worked very hard for this win; it was their forty-third
game of the season and we're still in February. Gerhard will not be
happy with his lot tonight as we head home to Wales and Rodgers
confirms the body blow that was Vorm's non-inclusion, citing the
reason as sickness. We can only hope he returns asap, as without
him we looked fragile in defence, and fragile in the defensive
build-up as well. I shouldn't be too disappointed because we are
back in fourteenth – I like it here – and on thirty points still, we are
three wins above last-placed QPR and Blackburn before relegation
gets really interesting with Bolton and Wigan both on twenty points
apiece. I also sense Martinez is plotting a resurgence in his team's
fortunes and if he is successful he will surely be manager of the
season. The two Manchester teams win, as do Chelsea against an
awful Bolton and Spurs get a hammering at Arsenal.

I hear Ashley Williams turned down a trip today to Downing
Street to represent football at a dinner with the prime minister, a
dinner to herald St David's Day which is being held on 29 February

(which is not St David's Day). The reason for Ash declining is obvious to all Welsh football fans; he will be on international duty at the Gary Speed memorial match in Cardiff against Costa Rica. Maybe the Prime Minister thought they would move the game for him?

Curtis Obeng, a young man signed from Wrexham and by all accounts a promising defender, has a disappointing start to his Swans career against Aston Villa reserves at Llanelli. A 2–0 defeat was a harsh introduction for him. He seems pleased though with his new club, and Swansea City have once again set aside a player and given him time to flourish at the highest level, albeit in the reserves. Alan Curtis is one hell of a mentor as well. Obeng would do well to listen to him – a quality coach who has been there and done it all before. Alan is another man who can be firmly put in the 'clubman' bracket. He professionally represents the club at all times, never confrontational and always amiable and happy to help.

At the end of a month that has again seen the side scrapping for every goal and point, I look at the remaining fixtures and it hits home that the thirty-eight-game Premier League season is not only a lot shorter than other leagues, but that your nineteen home games on a season ticket costing in excess of £400 are valuable. So valuable it hurts when you miss the odd game, and with ten weeks of the season left I don't intend to miss a kick.

The ides of March are upon us. The end of winter maybe?

Chapter Eleven

March:
Forward into Battle

'Psycho killer on the loose again, demented brain in constant pain', my iPod lurches in to life to the sound of the English Dogs as I look ahead to a real battle at the JJB today. Wigan away doesn't hold the 'grudge element' it did for certain Swansea fans last season when we travelled there on a midweek night with 5,000 fans in tow. Today there are thousands here, and Wigan are still so desperate for a win that you can feel the tension in the air. The inclusion of Gylfi in the line-up is becoming a must, as much as Leon Britton and Michel Vorm's names are on the team sheet every game we play. These sorts of players are a constant in all successful teams, the artist and the writer, each pulling strings while the keeper at the back conducts matters in a very competent manner. We will need some craft today as well, as Wigan have turned their fortunes around slightly since they were languishing at the foot of the table on fifteen points just a few weeks ago, and Martinez, a shrewd and clever manager, is steering them to another hyper end of season. In at number two is Graeme Jones, a man offered Brendan Rodgers' job and turning it down, before the Northern Irishman took the reins. I am not too sure he is the man for any number one position, he seems happier in the background taking on those team tasks which the manager doesn't want to be involved in. At Swansea Jones was the hard man, the disciplinarian, while Martinez was more thoughtful in his managerial style. At Bristol Rovers I recall Jones launching an attack on an opposition player and getting into a bit of bother for his efforts. I know as well that players at Swansea at the time were slightly fearful of Jones and his ability to discipline any player if that needed to be done. I am beginning to wonder how that took place . . . actually I know, but Jones is a quality act and with

Martinez they have the qualities to once again take Wigan right to the wire.

Andre Marriner warms up with his co-officials before the game and any match he is involved in gets me slightly nervous – he seems to be developing a track record in Swansea games for a bit of controversy. We really do need to go in search of our third away win to at least shut the press up with their 'worst away record' headlines every time we play. It would also give us a bit of space once again in the mid-table scrap-athon.

I maybe shouldn't have been that worried; throughout the 90 minutes at no point did I feel we were under threat or in any way in trouble. The away game at Stoke is clearly behind us and anyone who harbours fears of a repeat of our recent away form should relax now. Our possession football was quicker, and in the middle of the park we had total control, Nathan again displaying to a watching crowd why he should be included in the England side come the summer. He was dynamite. He was hard in the tackle and tricky with the ball at his feet – that was until Marriner, as I feared, decided to get involved and send him off. The clown today wasn't the referee, though, it was one Jordi Gomez, once again diving like a shot dog in a fair challenge by Dyer. His theatrics were unprofessional to say the least, and Marriner, clearly not an astute judge, decided a red card was his only option. Maybe he doesn't like flair football, or maybe Nathan was too quick for him to keep up with so he decided to even things up? It did for a while but this day in the warming March sunshine was Swansea City's and not even Andre Marriner could change that. He was a homer all day, and if it wasn't for his persistent involvement (we pay to see players not refs), the Swans would have increased the scoreline. Marriner, if nothing else, is very good at spoiling games of competitive football.

Right at the end of the half Gylfi took control of matters and shot home a delightful goal from twenty-odd yards to give the Swans a deserved 1–0 lead at the break. And even though a fifteen-minute verbal kicking from Martinez and Jones was dealt out to the players, a spectacular effort from a dead-ball situation gave the Swans the points. Gylfi most certainly was now growing to be the darling of the Swans supporters and his away displays are becoming legendary, if I dare use that word. Two more goals notched up for the Icelander. Wigan did rally and had a few chances at the end but in no way did they deserve anything at all against a fully functioning, combative and professional Swansea City side. Getting off the thirty point-mark was good for us as well. Although the league position tonight hasn't changed, it does put a good eleven points between the club and relegation. Liverpool are beginning to stutter as well, shipping goals where they usually wouldn't. A 2–1 home defeat to Arsenal and wins for the Manchester clubs start to distance the top two from the rest. Fulham's 5–0 thrashing of Wolves, with ex-Jack Terry Connor in charge at Molineux, served notice on Swansea they are no slouches at home – and they are coming up on the radar for us as a fixture.

Gylfi Sigurdsson has lifted the club at the right time, a signing so timely he is seemingly perfect for Swansea City. He is a ball-winner in midfield and able to instrument opportunities from any given situation. His grafting and workmanlike style, coupled with a certain degree of panache, is just what we need at the Liberty. I see Brendan Rodgers as key to him sealing the deal. It has been a strange week where Wales played a memorial match for Gary Speed, a tough and difficult time for his two sons who acted with great decorum in the full glare of the media. At Swansea we have started a month of madness, pure March madness, with sprinklings of Gylfi magic that earned us a 2–0 win at Wigan. I am sure – very, very sure – there is much more to come.

It's good as the first week comes to an end that Alan Tate is featuring again in training and even though we will not be appealing Nathan's three-game ban for his red at Wigan, we do have Wayne Routledge itching to prove a point or two in his absence. It is paramount for us as a club that players like Wayne come in and want to make a difference and take their opportunities. Leroy is an obvious player in this category given his recent absence from the first team, but Luke Moore – when he has been given the opportunity – has shown a lot of prowess in front of goal and links in well no matter where he is asked to play off the bench. Leroy has also been fined by the club a month after his arrest in London for being drunk and disorderly, and since then has struggled a bit to find his form.

Leroy was also arrested while at Middlesbrough a few years ago, and his recent failing outside the Mayfair Hotel in London, a celebrity hangout, will not please Brendan Rodgers. It takes our eyes off all the good work the club is doing. Leroy is quick to apologise and is quickly fined two weeks' wages. Quite right.

It's moments like that for players like Leroy that can mean another tick in the 'end of season transfer' box. I can't see the club tolerating this behaviour now the profile of the city is so good in the eyes of the football world. Leroy is a player I like, he has a hard edge, but he doesn't seem to have made his mark as I expected since signing for us, and his early-season goals are a distant memory. Anyway, less of the negative because we have a date with fate, and Manchester City on the horizon, a team that we are told will easily sweep us aside. I wonder. They are the best competitive side in the league but I will challenge their ability to scrap out a decent result at places like Swansea.

Ex-Manchester City player Neil Taylor is in the press this week, talking about having no grudges towards the club which released him as a youngster. Well, that may be so, but Neil will be an automatic pick for the weekend's game and can give them a bit of a slap if he has a mind to do so. The Swansea weather is picking up big time with record temperatures recorded in the Bay for the time of year and across the country. It seems the hot house that is the Premier League is affecting all of us. I hear all the predictions from all the 'experts' people like ex-footballer and Talksport talker of complete rubbish – Micky Quinn. Now here is a man who never listens, he clearly has had no media training or if he has he didn't listen. His interviews are absolutely pathetic, no planning, just spouting and shouting people down time and time again. He seems to be a radio host with little time for anyone else but himself. I love the way, too, that his prison term for drink driving wasn't his fault (maybe the voices made him do it?). A great goalscorer he was, but he should have got a proper job when he gave up football. So your opinion, no matter how many times you shout 'Listen, listen!' before you start a sentence, is null and void. The man who references members of the opposite sex as 'birds' and proudly talks of 'having four birds on the go' to boost his ego is the very worst breed of person in football. I hate them. There is lots more I could say about him, but I'll keep them for when I'm face-to-face with him. Honestly some people need taking down a peg or two. My weekly hate rant is over, but I am now so angry, why do I listen to people like this?

There will be a few opinionated football people shut up today. That's the fine opinion of Howard of Cowbridge and many others in the pub pre-match. The talk is of Manchester City having to just turn up and play to gain the three points, but surely the media are not that daft? Surely Swansea City have struck them blow after blow this season every time they attempted to predict the future? Brendan remains calm and confident, a man secure in the knowledge that he has done all he can to prepare the team for this big, big game. There is little more he or any of us can do now as the game kicks off in front of a TV audience of millions on a warm and balmy Sunday afternoon. The only thing left in our arsenal is to roar and sing, cheer and applaud the super Swans as we go for Citeh's jugular, and rip it to shreds.

More importantly, if we can upset the odds today and take down these overpaid monsters then we will have thirty-six points in the bag and may even be one win from certain safety, something that many predicted would not happen. The way we started the game gave us all a lot of hope, straight away opening up the millionaires' defence time and time again with Routledge tearing strips off his marker and eventually earning a penalty which Scott Sinclair failed to convert. Hart's save was good, but Scotty will not be happy with the way he took the penalty. It was his first penalty miss for Swansea. Danny Graham had chances, as did Gylfi as the headlines were being put on hold while the Swans tore in to the City defence throughout the first half. Mario Balotelli, the man who is everything to many and for me, everything I hate about footballers and their trade, doesn't get his own way and kicks the ball away, referee Mason decided to do nothing. Balotelli raged at the man in charge, and again Mason did nothing as Manchester City's ridiculous players and pathetic attitude was on show before us all. They were falling apart. The crowd jeered them and shouted, anger and laughter on their faces. The players become involved in that as well, smiling and gesturing at the crowd, this City side have lost it today; they are not in the zone and are ready to be taken.

I see Mancini gesturing and complaining like a spoilt boy; he hates not getting his own way the man in his light blue scarf, waving and shouting at things he sees as wrong – at things he can't control. If he were to be honest with himself for five minutes this season it should be now, and that honesty would say very clearly, 'My players are not good enough today, they are being taught a football lesson, and I don't like it.' Manchester City have two players who cost as much as our stadium; how greedy is that? This club want the title I know, but they will be buying it if they do win the league this season. What is looking certain though is they won't be getting three points today. It's now just a matter of time before they are dealt the final blow – surely ?

The second half was slightly more even, but even the most zealous City fan will say they were still second best. They increase their movement forward, though, with Kolo Touré, captain for the day, instrumental at times. He is a handful. Balotelli dives in the penalty area which shows how desperate this mercenary is today and then Joe Allen snatches at a shot that he could have done better with. Then Brendan makes a timely change. Seeing a tired Danny Graham almost out on his feet, the introduction of Luke Moore sees an instant change. From a corner Moore heads his first touch with power straight into the back of the Manchester City net. Hart was nowhere near it. It was almost as if we expected it to come as the players surround Luke Moore to celebrate a cracking goal to put the Swans one up. Then a piece of excellent decision-making from linesman/second official? er, assistant ref? Sian Massey. As Manchester City desperately pushed forwards Micah Richards was offside. Picking up on the situation she raised her flag as he hit his shot into the back of the net – the Swans at last this season on the right side of a good decision. Thank you Sian for your professionalism.

The game ended with Manchester City out on their feet and a jubilant Swansea side celebrating with each other and then the crowd. Days like this are indeed what it is all about; victories like this are the reason why we go, and the reason why we spend half our lives, following, supporting and talking about football. The result was a fair one, and a well-fought one that catapults Swansea City once again to the forefront of everyone's minds. The morons who fought outside (Manchester City inspired jealousy at their loss) are laughable, but some watch as a few fences are attacked so the fighting few can force their will on each other. You can guarantee that had Manchester City won the game they wouldn't have behaved in that way, and as ever Swansea have those who oblige such actions and will participate fervently. It is quite sad. Stanley

Collymore reports the win and at last sees the side of our football that matters. At last he concentrates on what we have done, not what the opposition didn't do, and at last he looks further than the end of his nose to report on the game. Radio Wales are as quiet as ever, so we tune in for the Radio 5 live phone-in as we travel back to Gloucester. The nation is in shock that Swansea could do such a thing. The result also signifies the toppling of Manchester City from the top of the table, with Manchester United taking their place as the season rolls onwards. We now have thirty-six points and are on the best form of the season, seemingly unstoppable as we head towards May and safety. Brendan talks post-match and states that 'the best team won' and although he respected the opposition, we very much deserve all the credit we get. The players are referred to as 'courageous' and he says that Manchester City had to make tactical changes because of the fact that Swansea played so well. Sometimes there is little else to say after a game like this. The Sunday drive home was easy, the few beers once there easier, and the week ahead felt like it was going to be a doddle.

This week there is a Barclays league survey and have a guess who came out on top as the most impressive Premier League manager? It goes without saying, doesn't it? Brendan is now being talked about for other jobs and other challenges. And as we have already talked about its clear the bigger clubs like what they see, especially when they look at what they have got. The Everton fixture later on in the month has sold out and the uptake for Swansea tickets is incredible, The ground expansion is back on the lips of a lot of Welsh football folk. Regardless of the current maximum of 20,600 or so, it clearly isn't enough to satisfy the desire of the nation to follow Wales' top side. Much has been said about this and the overall stadium expansion relies upon success, and how this is gauged. Is it clear it should be now? However, with clubs like Brighton expanding to over 30,000 capacity and Norwich battening down the hatches to clear 25,000 most games, if there is a need for a quick decision on Swansea's capacity increase, it is now.

The Swans are currently on a roll of good results after Manchester City and the stunning win at Wigan – now we move onwards to Fulham. It's a great place to watch football is Craven Cottage. A place of history and regardless of the ridiculous statue of Michael Jackson outside, it is a ground many have enjoyed a good day out at. Martin Jol has rallied his side of late with some great results so Saturday's trip will possibly be the hardest away test for some time. I would settle for a point now, but we are so close to that magical thirty-nine point barrier that perhaps should we go all out and take risks for the three points today?

Many clubs have been battered at the Cottage this season; Wolves took one hell of a pelting there and today with a decent weather forecast and a huge Swans support adding to the atmosphere, it could be a cracker. There is a neutral area at Fulham, in which I know many Jacks will be – watching the Swans in London is a special day out. We have suffered greatly at this ground and at times it has been an unlucky place for us to visit, you can be caught out quickly here, and all the top clubs have fallen here in recent years, let alone 'relegation candidates' like us.

There hasn't been much in the way of top-flight football this week, though the Merseyside derby saw a 3–0 Liverpool win. With only two games in the Premier League today we will feature heavily on tonight's *Match of the Day*. Saturdays in London are special. The matchday atmosphere is probably lost on many of the capital's fans, but a visit here is very, very unique. For many the Cottage is their favourite ground to visit, and the sun in the sky signals a decent feeling about the whole affair down by the river.

I expected an onslaught of the Martin Jol variety today but it never came, not at all – not once did we feel the pressure that Wolves did, or QPR at the start of the month. The free-flowing style of our delicious team's play is complete and total football. The Swans' pass-and-move play hypnotises the Fulham boys as they become bit-part players in the game itself. Once the initial 5 minutes or so was over and Vorm had denied Fulham two opportunities, the game was Swansea City's to take. Over the first 20 minutes there were a few chances for Danny Graham and Scott Sinclair as Leon started to probe and create opportunities for willing runners Gylfi and Routledge. Joe Allen was also pulling the strings as Rangel and Taylor moved forward to support attacks, so it really was just a matter of time before we broke Fulham's resolve.

The goal came just before half time as Gylfi finished off some good Sinclair work, a deserved goal though by that time we could have scored three. Riise at the back for Fulham didn't look at all happy and the poor Senderos and all-over-the-place Diarra looked as if they'd be happy to get back into the dressing room for some respite. Pavel Pogrebnyak, Fulham's newly acquired striker, was non-existent. He was a player I had been concerned about before the game, but I suppose if you haven't got the ball it's pretty difficult to score. The absence of Ashley Williams through illness was not an issue . . . we could have played with two at the back and still won this game.

The second half started as the first half finished, with Swansea City crawling all over the Fulham midfield and back four. Resistance seemed to be futile and the continual passing movements of the orange-shirted Jacks fired the away support into magnificent voice. This was turning out to be the away performance of the season. There were periods in this game in which Fulham could not get anywhere near the ball. One passing move went on for approximately 70 seconds and resulted in the goal of the season for me. It won't get the award; it was a passing masterclass finished off by that man again – Gylfi. The Swans are flying. 2–0 up and the songs from the noisy fans echo around an otherwise quiet and outfought Fulham team and their even weaker support. Joe Allen added a third, and Scotty could have bagged two more, as could Leon.

The Swans were victorious again, and I would say Fulham, out on their feet and devoid of any ideas in the face of this onslaught, were clueless to do anything but admire our display. It was absolutely flawless – 60 per cent possession away from home and Swansea City cruise in to eighth place in the Premier League. Over 25,000 people watched this performance, and many stayed behind from the home side to show their appreciation of the Swansea team as they left the field. Afterwards the comments on the radio were very appreciative, and to some extent expected. The Swans fans on the journey home to all corners of the UK would have been so happy to hear that the football world has now heard very much indeed about our wonderful first season in the Premier League.

Fabrice Muamba 'died' on the pitch at Spurs an hour or so later in an FA Cup tie playing for Bolton. News circulates that evening that he collapsed and had to be resuscitated by medical teams to no avail as he left the pitch. News also circulates that he was dead for over an hour before he was finally revived. If that turns out to be true what an amazing feat from those brilliant people who saved his life when many would surely have given up. Fortunately a consultant cardiologist was in the crowd and assisted staff on the pitch as Muamba was taken to hospital and had defibrillator treatment to attempt to restart his heart. As I write this he is in intensive care, and not a lot of hope is being given for any recovery at all. It's football that drives me mad at times and also takes me to the strongest feelings of emotion and passion at any given time, and tonight on a dusty March evening it also delivers a sharp reminder about how fragile all this is, that life can be lost in the blink of an eye. Yours, mine and anyone we know; children, friends and colleagues. I am quite harsh at times, but really deep down I know as much as anyone how lucky we all are tonight to be safe, secure and at home with the family.

The super Swans are on a roll. Wolves get battered 5–0 at home by Manchester United who are now eyeing the title and kicking out behind them at a startled Manchester City who have Chelsea as visitors this coming Wednesday. Arsenal will have to gain all three points as well at Everton. Swansea City now have four away wins to add to the points tally of thirty-nine and many now are talking about a European place again. Is this all real? Can we really handle a European journey at Swansea next season? Thursday games and loads of them, as well as preserving this holy Premier League grail? It's incredible. Utter madness.

Garry Monk must be wondering what is going on as well. After a very solid performance alongside Stephen Caulker at Fulham (owing to Ash's sickness) he reports in the press of his amazement on how his career has panned out. He has been with us for some time, and could have been a mere speck on the football map, but today as we head towards the third week of March 2012, he is club captain of a Premier League football team. Could he ever have imagined this in his wildest dreams? With Everton at home our next fixture at the Liberty and Lee Trundle getting in on the media frenzy, all eyes this week will be on Swansea's tremendous progression to eighth place and looking right up the backsides of the so-called big names. There are a few who won't like this at all.

Manchester City defeat Chelsea and Arsenal soften up Everton for us and grab an away win at Goodison in midweek. That ensures that I and the rest of our hardy crew are more than confident that

Saturday's game in a pretty packed Premier League programme could well see us go on even further. As the season gets businesslike, so does my writing style. I become more effective and productive with over 100,000 words already penned for editing and three books full of notes and quotes documenting travels and experiences; the final seven weeks will be a tough task, that's for sure. Creativity is never right at your fingertips, those of you who do this far better than me will wake up in the middle of the night and quickly scribble ideas that in the cold light of day look like a drunk man's grumble. This happens to me as well and as much as I look to Swansea City for inspiration, I also look to my family for support. It isn't easy producing a document such as this and it takes its toll. Working and travelling, watching football and the writing, not to mention my band, are massive commitments and give little time for much else. I am lucky indeed. The game against Everton will signal the end of the month as the Tottenham game is on Sky now that they love the Swansea style. This means another Sunday journey for the travelling Jacks. It is a fact that we have never beaten Everton in a league game, and over the time I have followed the Swans we have rarely looked like changing that stat. The pre-Christmas game where we were bored to within an inch of our lives and suffered another loss gives me no comfort at all. Today's game is as good a chance as ever that we can reverse this horrible stat once and for all.

The game itself was another poor capitulation that reflected a tired Swansea side going through the motions against a rampant and effective Everton team. For those who hoped of European glory . . . well, that idea may be slightly further away after a 2–0 defeat at home to a quality performance from Everton. Inspired by Leighton Baines and a terrific free kick and their general domination over the 90 minutes meant the Toffees totally deserved the three points. Their new signing Nikica Jelavic is a tremendous player, too; he has a good eye for goal and could have scored four easily. The answer from Swansea were few and far between owing to the high tempo set by Everton and a very decent pressing tactic from manager David Moyes. The Swans had little answer to this and try as we might through Joe Allen and Danny Graham, our goal today was out of reach. It was a game that finished as it started with Everton battering down the door. Fair play to them, they have bounced back after some dodgy results, and where better this season to make noise than at Swansea City. This is the freestyle play we are used to inflicting on sides, not being on the receiving end of. Moyes had done his homework well and had taken some heat out of some of his dissenters' voices; his team had worked hard for him and done the club proud.

I travelled home disappointed and hurting quite badly, not from the result but from the pain in my chest. It was horrible. We all feel out of sorts at times and I put this down to my age and the hard travelling I have done of late. Little did I know that I was about to go on a long journey too, and it would be as terrifying a journey that I have ever been on.

Chapter Twelve

April and May: Don't go Breaking my Heart

A pril is a time when a lot of amateurish pundits make Talk Sport-style predictions. OK they have been making them all season, but now they make some real mistakes. All they seem to see is the latest result – not the bigger picture. The reason for this is that we are dealing with people with little if any decent training in any job other than kicking a ball. Sometimes fans gets stick from the professional footballers. They say things like, 'They have never played the game, what do they know?' Well I say, ask Arsène Wenger, for all his moaning he is a successful manager who hardly kicked a ball. So in response I say 'They haven't ever had a proper job, so what gives them the right to judge me?' I also think that media training in communication, the ability to verbalise their thoughts and project their voices appropriately wouldn't go amiss either. Our away game at QPR has been moved to the Wednesday after Easter for Sky (the love-in continues), so after Good Friday and a home tie against Newcastle (also on Sky) we have a weekend that delivers some mouth-watering games.

The definitive ties are Wolves v Bolton, QPR v Arsenal and Blackburn v Manchester United. These games will throw up losers and they may well be the losers at the end of the season in the relegation mix. The Swans travel to Tottenham for a Sunday game (live on Sky – oh yes, kerching Mr Levy!), and a huge test in North London, far bigger than the Arsenal test that's for sure. On the evening before the Tottenham game I feel like shit, really ill, and decide that as it's on the TV I will remain at home. This settles m

down a bit but between you and me I haven't felt like this before . . .
I feel all drowsy and disinterested with the odd shooting pain in my
head and lower back. I don't feel on the ball at all.

I make notes, watch the game and make some more notes, the
fever getting worse as I attempt to analyse then document the one-
way traffic that was our away defeat at Tottenham. The start of each
half may well have given us some hope, especially another goal from
the dynamic Gylfi, but overall we struggled, making errors at crucial
times and capitulated to a 3–1 loss. Goals from van der Vaart and
Adebayor sorted us out and once we had conceded the second to
go 2–1 down, for me it was inevitable. The Swans supporters were
magnificent though, a squeezed-in echoing noise around White Hart
Lane, Welsh dragons on fire, real dragons with real passion. Sadly,
and this may have been down to my illness, I couldn't muster that
much passion for the game, and went to bed early.

Two days later I was in intensive care in Gloucestershire Royal
Hospital hanging on to consciousness and wired up to machines.
The pain had been replaced with surges of lightning and flashes
which I would describe as a torrid, ripped-up and tearing collision
that produced stinging punches to my chest. I was, to all concerned,
having a heart attack. The words 'tachycardia' and 'fibrillation'
were being muttered as a poor guy next to me passed away on
the small wheelie bed he was unconscious on. With all the drama
unfolding I thought this was it, I don't mind telling you. My heart
rate then increased to 150 beats per minute and the doctor said
that this is normal and I should be relieved, though I needed some
control methods introduced to make the irregular rhythms more
acceptable and reduce the pain. He diagnosed *atrial fibrillation*,
not a heart attack. He tells me this is good compared to a heart
attack and the ECG had displayed a condition not that common,
but manageable – *for the rest of my life*. For the next few days
cardiologists came and went as did students, doctors, machines and
CT scans. Calcium scores and heart reflection is measured and I feel
a bit like I have been poked and prodded enough. There are good
things that happen when you are in these types of situations. One
would be that you find out who your mates are, while another is
that you actually get time to reflect on your life, and what it is you
have done, and maybe would very much like to do later on. I find
out quite a few things and over the next three days I am worked

upon and released back in to the community with beta blockers (a pill in the pocket) and further visits planned to eminent folk with qualifications far greater than I will ever obtain. My own personal game is on as well. The good news is the old ticker is as strong as an ox, though the fags have to go and maybe a bit more careful thought should be put into my food and alcohol intake. Yes, all the things we all love, gone in a flash. The missus is well pleased.

On the Thursday of the same week I look at the game the next day, that Good Friday game against Newcastle, and good old Andy drives the happy crew, and me –the Jack invalid – down Swansea way.

You honestly didn't think that I wouldn't make it did you? My cardiologist suggests a bit of time off work, to relax and do the things I want to do as opposed to what everyone else wants me to do. The demands, some self-induced, have to be placed to one side (so the band immediately take a year off, the USA again placed on hold) and I concentrate on a leisurely lifestyle for a month or so. I am quite pleased to hear it to be honest. I am prescribed some pills that control the heart and ensure the episodes will not return, and this, my friends is about as much as I want to write about this condition. All I will say is that it is very hard to diagnose, and I was lucky – many people die from these events and the fact my heart was so strong enabled me to hang on as the specialist work was done that evening in the busy Gloucestershire Royal Hospital. We put our lives in to the hands of these young people, the medication and dedication is taken for granted, and there is no more sudden jolt to the system than being in an intensive care ward with people expiring around you. I now will take pills for the rest of my life, and if I am lucky an eminent chap from the John Radcliffe in Oxford will perform a heart op that will rid me of the condition by inserting a needle into the main artery in my leg, which will travel through my body and burn away the damaged tissue surrounding my heart, so damaged that it is determined to kill me. There is a small success rate with this, and there is a small fatality rate as well. I will continue to be in a quandary for some months to come.

There are small mercies though, I am nearly fifty, with plenty o scrapping qualities, and this fight is one I intend to win. I am now back at work, fighting the worst in people as ever, and fronting every situation that is presented to me with no fear and plenty o compassion. That is the best I can do, and the best I can hope for. Yes, there are major life changes but they can be achieved, and as normal a life as possible can be achieved as well. The game, as I said, is on.

The Newcastle game is featured strongly via media outlets as we travel to see the Swans turn around a few dodgy results. Yes, we all know the foot has been taken off the pedal somewhat, with our Premier League destiny achieved easily, but this should not take away our desire to win games and compete at every level as the season ends.

Brendan Rodgers' stock value has never been so high and our discussions range from him leaving (when) to where he will go (and when) and how that will affect us as a club. I think the main topic is when he will go, for me it goes without any doubt that Brendan will almost certainly leave the club, my hope is that he will give us another season or so before making that move. He is a man with many qualities, and integrity I see as one of them, although he his making no promises which concerns me somewhat. My very good contacts in the game and outside the Swansea boundary tell me that he is on the wish list of a number of clubs, and all of them are bigger than Swansea. By that they don't means the silly clubs like Cardiff, nor the struggling Sheffield United who languish scrapping for a play-off place in League One. No, they mean the big clubs and by this I am told the top six. Premier League. Proper big clubs, not Birmingham City, who think they are big, nor Cardiff who keep saying they are big (and they believe it – click your heels Dorothy and follow the yellow brick road).

Newcastle are not one of those clubs, but in the bawling, uneducated management style that shouts and bullies on the touchline they do have some luck in Alan Pardew. He hasn't got the grace of Rodgers, nor the longevity I am sure that football brings with it for true professionals, but my word does he have a good scouting system. It may be the club's ability or it may be his, but this is a *real* quality. If it is Pardew, and I have my doubts, he should be on a lawful percentage (like other managers have tried, albeit illegally) because the club has some real gems on board. The Geordies take to the pitch as the East Stand summons help for a poor chap who is taken very ill as the game starts. The booming 'Hymns and Arias' and the loud and constantly cheering support get behind the side who are sluggish from the off. This 'Premier League survival is a done deal' scenario has already taken a hold after just a minute. We have to be on our game here. Newcastle have in Cissé a real gem of a player, while Cabaye and Ben Arfa ooze quality. Tiote prods and probes almost Britton-like and Ba is a dream; they have quality everywhere. *It only takes 5 minutes for the first goal to go in as Dyer hit a thirty-yard screamer into the top corner of the net; the first of five goals for the Swans in a magnificent celebratory day which has started so well. . . .*

But of course it doesn't happen like that. It never does, when you're going to get spanked, like Everton did to us, then you are going to get spanked. That's the way it is folks, and although we can dream, there was no Dyer screamer, or Danny Graham winner this time. No Gylfi free kick or Vorm penalty-save. It was Newcastle's day and we slowly conceded ground, the ball and then territory as defeat was forced upon us. Again like Everton it could have been more but the qualities we do have are of a battling nature. No team will hammer us this season, so we go to Plan B and defend our hearts out. It's time for the back four to show the spirit that came so easily as the season has progressed. They do so, and the rear-guard action, for the connoisseur, is a pleasure to see. The fighting spirit this time comes from Ashley Williams and Rangel, Neil Taylor and Stephen Caulker. Moore came on and helped out a beleaguered and battered side that through all the displays of character was most certainly going to lose the game.

The omission from the starting line-up of Scott Sinclair and Danny Graham, only brought on when the game was lost, may well have been a fault, but the manager knows his players and maybe they needed the rest after a long and demanding season. The use of some fresh faces occasionally works, but not today. Joe tried to make amends with a stunning strike but we still lost even with 68 per cent of the possession (yes, we lost the game and were dominated, but had 68 per cent of the possession!). At the end of the 90 minutes we had nothing to show for it.

Papiss Cissé was magnificent; a player who finds room where there is none and creates opportunity where none can be seen took centre stage. In front of the travelling support he created what I believe will be the goal of the season – surely nobody will equal or beat this finish? The way he curved his shot and his body round the ball to beat an advancing Vorm will go down as one of the best goals the Liberty has seen. For all the Trundle magic and unbelievable strikes, this matches them. What a goal! The game is won, however we need to take some solace from our battling belief that we could take something from the game. To the end we fought and passed and moved and to the end we refused to die and concede defeat. The battle cry is still a loud one. We had nineteen strikes on goal throughout, and this signifies a never-say-die and a desire not to let the fans down. I am pleased tonight for many reasons, personally and for the Swans; we lost but we lost well if that makes sense?

I'm in and out of hospital for tests as the QPR away game on a blustery Wednesday night in London comes and goes – I watched it though, and this was a performance we all don't want to see repeated. The loss as the QPR fans bawled 'Boring, Boring, Swansea!' was the worst performance of the season, and should be placed firmly into the category 'forget it'. It was one of those games that we all as fans don't want to talk about. The capitulation at Loftus Road for the nation to laugh at was appalling. The players apologise immediately as they know the extent of their failure. The travelling thousands don't deserve this; no supporter should see their team fall so quickly after conceding a goal. The final score is 3–0. We never do well in this part of London and as the night falls I get text messages which I feel blame me for the loss; among others 'Where are you?' and 'Oi, plastic, where are you mush?' are sent. Yeah, yeah, yeah – I wish I could be there but I am doing an impression of *Alien* all wired up and bleeping. Apparently my life is more important to my family than an away game at QPR. So, Mr Shankly, it turns out you were wrong. Life is more important and though all of us cling to hope in one way or another (and football is a source of hope through the emotions it provokes), life, I can tell you, is there to cherish. I look at my grandson, and know this is true.

In a week where Tony Pennock took the young Swans to glory in the Welsh Cup and Joe Allen makes the apologies for a miserable Wednesday in London, he is followed by many more, including the manager. What a team needs when this happens is a quick fix – a game to come quickly to exorcise the misery. This is granted as Blackburn linger on the horizon with their hugely popular manager Steve Kean at the helm. How he is still there I do not know. The side has rallied of late but a loss against Swansea will see them dead certs for the drop. In true Hollins style Kean does not accept this. 'Judge me at the end of the season,' he says. OK Steve, even us Jacks have heard that before. That is the statement of a dying man, a lost prophet signalling a club's demise. The level of away support at the Liberty this weekend tells me that many have lost hope and given up on Blackburn's cause.

We have a group of games coming up that can restore some faith and belief in the team before the big ending to the season: Manchester United away and Liverpool at home. Our recent losses after such an inspiring run quickly affect some fans who scream for scapegoats. These fans, I think, are those who are being called 'Plastics' on the internet. I am not sure if all of them are, but they seem to be the new breed, who clearly do not have much recall from ten years before, or if they do they have little knowledge as to what was done back then that brings us here today. I say this because if they did they would have some measured recollection of certain games, and two home defeats do not signal the end of the voyage for the Golden Fleece, it just instigates positive investigation and inspires the team to do better. OK, the QPR game was a debacle, a real nonsense of a game that should never be repeated, no matter what level we are at in the future. But it was a one-off, of that much I am sure. And anyway, with Kean's whipping boys on the horizon, faith can easily be restored. Then the doom merchants can crawl back under their rocks for a bit.

Eddie May died yesterday, he was a man I remember more as the manager of Cardiff City than a bustling Swans defender. Tributes roll in as both sides of the Welsh football divide commiserate and display their emotions as to who Eddie was and what he achieved as a football man. He had a fine sense of humour on camera. I recall one occasion at Ninian Park when the away support in its thousands berated him during a poorly timed interview with the BBC after a Swans victory. He smiled, waved and took it well. Eddie died in his sleep at the age of sixty-eight. He even managed my home town club at the Bridge Meadow, Haverfordwest. It's again a thoughtful moment for me as death rears its ugly head. We all have an inevitable conclusion, even those of us who think ourselves indestructible.

Today we need a classy performance, a proper display that matches our Swansea propaganda. We must not falter as a scrapping Blackburn, in need of every goal and point, will almost certainly present itself before us. Players like N'zonzi and Yakubu will be firing on all cylinders today surely? The weather is getting better as well and the Swans take centre stage at their very own centre stage, the Liberty Stadium. For me, and I think many others, the manager takes no chances today; we field our strongest side with every player a winner for the side this season. If Blackburn are to win today it will be well deserved. It's the midfield dominance which has been sparked by Gylfi in the latter stages of the season that has won key games for us. This is the story today, the Swansea triangle is back! The confidence and spark returns and the ball is our friend again as we pass and move and dictate all matters football to a headless Blackburn side. In games like this, no matter who the opposition is – be it Liverpool or Wolves, Blackburn, Manchester City or Arsenal – you're not winning the game.

Steve Kean is not a Premier League tactician – he can't be, his side are lost, they have no fight in them at all and the inevitable goal, a spectacular effort from Gylfi, gets the ball rolling. They had been warned several times already through Gylfi and Scott, so when he did score it was no surprise. But the quality of the strike was amazing – it could not have been struck better and Paul Robinson had no chance of saving it. Nathan Dyer added a second just before half time and the game for Blackburn, in a very similar vein to our home game against Everton, was very much over. Unless Kean could come up with some football magic to inspire the feet of Pedersen and Hoilett they were doomed. Blackburn looked like a side resigned to relegation, their fight was so gone that it didn't even come on the bus with them. Or indeed, perhaps it was that the Swans were so good, so effective, that Blackburn were not going to be good enough? We made them look League One standard, because to say they looked Championship is an insult to all but a few sides at that level.

Mark Clattenburg had little to do but book Hoilett and that well-known kitchen surface Formica to cap a miserable day for Blackburn Rovers. The third goal was inevitable and came from a defensive error from Scott Dann. The move, though, was sublime, with Scotty tearing down the pitch beating player after player before passing to Gylfi who hit the post with his effort. The rebound summed up Rovers' day (and season) and hit Dann to go over the line.

3–0 then, and the Swans are now on forty-two points after thirty-four games in the Premier League. There is no way now the club can be relegated this season, and the victory is celebrated as such. The players now know where they will be next season. The game ended with Lita missing an opportunity as well as a few other chances that fell the wrong side of the post. It could have been seven or eight, and if it had been nobody would have been surprised. David Dunn hit the post for Rovers in a rare venture forwards, but that was all that they could muster – they look doomed to the drop and the hangman's noose has tightened.

The fallout from the result is excellent, the TV pundits all expected a Swansea victory, and for us to be in the Premier League and beating sides as comprehensively as this is a dream.

Gylfi Sigurdsson reflected afterwards that the team spirit that he is experiencing at Swansea has never been matched by any club he has been at. His statement that he loves the city and fans is by the by – that is expected – but to look deeper into the psyche of the club in the way he has, shows a man who may well still be a Swansea City player come July. This all depends on the manager, a man who has already this season ruled himself out of the Chelsea job so surely this means he is focussed on Swansea and no other club, regardless of the suitors he will attract come May? We have had too many summers of discontent, even though the board have brilliantly appointed managers who have improved us on the pitch season after season (Sousa included); in Brendan we have an all-round tactician and communicator. A rare breed, a rare talent, and one that is admired everywhere.

An injury to Wayne Hennessy at Wolves has moved our Dorus into the number one jersey at Wolves which could mean we will see the Dutchman once again at the Liberty Stadium before the season ends. First up though it's Owen Coyle – another man in a desperate position. His Bolton side are also looking far from safe in the league and after a weekend of results which sees the Swans in twelfth, things are definitely somewhat rocky down Reebok way. Manchester United still head the table two points clear of Oasis City, despite a 6–1 hammering of Norwich; Arsenal are third easing past Wolves 3–0 at Molineux, while Manchester United win 4–0 against Villa. The goals are flying in. The end-of-season clash between City and United, even for me, is a mouth-watering prospect. I may even watch it!

Brendan Rodgers is now in full flow and the media gobble up a confident pre-match press chat before we move north again to Bolton. The old Twitter thing is at last making sense to me as well. The big names tweet and thousands follow; I send a tweet to a waiting world and a bloke in Dunstable tells me to 'fuck off and eat my own shit'. OK, well I haven't got as many followers as Stephen Fry yet, but . . . well, I will never have as many followers as Stephen Fry, but I would like a hundred by the end of the month. For whatever reason though, and I can't work it out, this Twitter thing is an infectious fad. I find myself drawn to a 'Bored Ghost', and a parody account of John Ruddy. Another is a 'Profanity Swan' in the north-east, who appears to be a chap wearing a t-shirt with 'wanker' written on it, with buffet food stuck all over his face. I love this, it's either really bad or sheer brilliance. And then there is 'Roy Cropper', laugh ? Oh yes.

Many Swans fans would settle for a draw at Bolton, but deep down Brendan will want to lay the ghost of that QPR result once and for all and so fields a strong side. This is in a week that sees Wigan turn over Arsenal at the Emirates to give them a morsel of hope, but it's the Swans who are in really confident mood. Having scored enough goals to satisfy these doom monger-types last week, a result at a blustery Bolton would indeed go down very well.

Scott Sinclair steadies the nerves early on with a decent goal putting us one up, and our play and stylish patterned movements all over the pitch has Bolton at sixes and sevens. Swansea are having a big say in who stays up and goes down, and like last week they tear shreds off the opposition. Somehow Gylfi and Danny Graham failed to convert chances before Chris Eagles drew Bolton level. It was against the run of play and the 3,000 Jacks in the crowd were stunned, for a few seconds at least. I have to say the booming songs which carried across the Bolton ground today were heart-warming. The fans of the home side cannot be heard; they are quiet and almost, like Blackburn, accepting of their fate. To say Bolton were living a charmed life is an understatement and to say that the Swans should have scored four in a completely controlled first half is not. Adam Bogdán in the Bolton goal kept them in the game as did furious defending from Steinsson and Ricketts. Ref Phil Dowd had little to do but admire the Swansea way.

The introduction of David Ngog inspired Bolton briefly, but the side at fault for not capitalising on the many chances created was definitely Swansea. Afterwards, as the points were shared and news comes through of a Blackburn win at Norwich, our Premier League rivals seem as down and out as Blackburn did the week before. Football fans react as to the next result and what is before them, much the same as some of the media do when they say a game in September is a Premier League decider. However, on this occasion those shattered Bolton fans leaving the Reebok are right, they are as deadbeat as they can be; they have also lost their fight and ability to win, and it shows all over the pitch. It just seems utter madness that we didn't knock Bolton for at least six.

More intriguing is the capitulation of Manchester United in a thrilling 4–4 draw at Old Trafford against Everton, following which Manchester City gain ground with a 2–0 win at long lost Wolves. The lead for United is now down to five points, but the title is theirs to lose. City's win determines Wolves' fate for next season; they are officially relegated and Terry Connor looks so lost and so upset at the confirmation of his club's future that he almost bursts in to tears. I feel as if we are heading for one of those end-of-season showdowns again; that crazy last Sunday of the season that affects relegation and promotion, champions and European destiny and which is ever-changing as the 90 minutes progresses. This season is coming to a tumultuous end.

All eyes are now focussed on the Premier League throughout the world, across the millions and millions of football fans' faces dance the majestic skills of Dyer and Sinclair, the prowess in midfield of Gylfi and the expertise and fluidity of Joe Allen. Now our stars in white shirts are known throughout the civilised world (and Cardiff). No man nor woman who follows this cherished game can deny that this has been a wonderful season for the flying Swans. The few results that have rattled us have seen a bigger and better side bounce back time and time again. We prove when hope seems lost that this Swansea way is the right way, and no hoof-ball tactic can beat us. To do so you need some genius as Moyes or character as Lambert, indeed the luck of Pardew as well. Ferguson scraped a win and Mancini was left bewildered. Wenger was just irritated but also left the Liberty a loser, in terms of his own conduct and the game itself. This Swansea style is ours and nobody can deny us that.

The visit of Wolves at the end of a productive and settling month brings with it my Twitter pal Graham Large from 'It's Round and it's White', an excellent website which gauges games through the real voices of football – the fans. He and his tribe of desperados make it to the Globe public house; Graham is a keen Wolves fanatic humble in his team's relegation and with him is a bloke called Dwarfio. They sup beers, find solace, and Graham announces his new team in the Premier League is indeed Swansea City. This game should hold no fears for us at all, as it won't hold any for the gold shirts of Wolverhampton. They are now free from their shackles; the chains are off, they are down and now have no pressure to perform and no requirement to get any result, because no result is expected.

Dorus features in goal for Wolves and to say he took more of a kicking than I have ever seen any keeper take this season in those first 30 minutes is an understatement. He was knocked out on the floor. It was to become of the craziest games witnessed at the Liberty since the Blackpool game at the end of a hectic season when we lost 6–3; this was pure entertainment. At the end the teams shared the points and eight goals, but there could have been twice that. Swansea City found themselves 4–1 up in the first half hour and if it wasn't for a second Wolves goal from Matt Jarvis on 33 minutes, this was set to be a landslide. Already ahead from goals by Orlandi after 20-odd seconds, then Joe Allen before 5 minutes was up, then Dyer and Graham, the Swans threatened to break records. Somehow Wolves stabilised themselves and even at 4–1 they felt they could get something from the game. The second goal from Jarvis fired them into a new phase of hope and suddenly they were on the ball.

The second half was mainly dominated by the gold and black and they scored two more goals to secure a point in a type of game that rarely features in the Premier League. However, Manchester United's 4–4 draw last week, equally as dramatic, will be met with claims of a poor Premier League, and poor players to boot. This, the most watched and expensive league in the world, will disagree. I, as a fan of a Premier League team, completely disagree; my journey this season watching us play every team in the league has been an education. This league spares no team which shows a weakness, and will punish severely any side that does not take its chances, or indeed those which gifts chances to the opposition. These are Premier League facts. The negativity generally comes with a twist of jealousy from those who still think that Charlton should be top class, or West Ham, Birmingham, Leeds or Wednesday. Yes, they are well-supported clubs in the main (not Charlton), but this does not make them good teams – you only need look at their league positions to find that out. West Ham may well gain promotion this season, but the way they fell from grace from a Premier League that is supposedly poor makes them truly awful.

At the end of April, a month for me which was life-changing, I have one more game to go to, and one more game to watch on TV. I gave up hope of a ticket for Manchester United away, and as much as I could have easily made a phone call and gained admission, I felt with my heart scare (and all that had gone before), if I was to die it would better if I were at home than in Manchester. Nothing personal . . . well, slightly personal, but don't worry. These are the two games we all feared we would have to win or at least take something from to stay in the league. Well, that myth is thankfully exploded and we have no fears as the last two weeks of the season hit us.

I laugh at QPR's capitulation – 6–1 at Chelsea as well. I will say this though, looking at their last few games they will probably stay up, but I hope they don't. The result of the weekend is Manchester City beating their near neighbours 1–0 to take the top spot in a timely manner. Both teams are on eighty-three points and City have the better goal difference. It will be a dramatic end to matters this time around, no doubt. Arsenal are firmly in third and Tottenham placed fourth. The fact that Chelsea are now in the Champions League final against Bayern means all Spurs fans will pray for a Bayern win. If Chelsea win, they will qualify for next season's competition as winners, and Spurs' fourth place will mean nothing, while if they lose then Spurs will qualify. It's a very strange game we follow. In the Fair Play stakes Swansea City are top of the league in England, and this means qualification for the Europa League, but only if you finish in the top three leagues of Fair Play and currently England are outside the top ten. It is very unlikely that the Swans will qualify for European football this time around, and it's fair to say I am more than happy with that. Yes, it would be a tremendous achievement to do so, but it brings with it too many challenges for such a newly promoted club in the Premier League, not to mention the expense for us all!

Mention has to be made of a fantastic goal by Papiss Cissé at Newcastle. Not content with scoring what may well have been goal of the season at the Liberty, he manages to score one of the most exhilarating goals ever seen in recent history when Newcastle beat Chelsea at Stamford Bridge on 2 May. In fact it goes down for me as one of the greatest Premier League goals of all time. The penultimate weekend to a tremendous and enthralling season is upon us, and as is traditional, the Swans are live on TV.

Andrea Orlandi's surprise inclusion against Wolves was an inclusion which sparked more than a bit of admiration from me, but it may well be his last appearance in a Swans shirt. Of course now that I've said that, he will surely sign a three-year deal next season! I was maybe a tad harsh on the young man from Spain in *Walking on Sunshine* (in fact he told me personally that he felt that I was), but if that criticism helped spark him out of his malaise then good. I'm not saying it did, but it's nice to have a point to prove, and prove it he did last week against Wolves. He has shone in all his starts this season – against Aston Villa and Wolves especially – and maybe he has a bit more to offer next season. I don't know too many Swans fans who will think the same, and he needs to be more involved when he gets the nod – a nod that he won't be getting against Manchester United, I am sure of that. Alan Tate is back from a niggling injury, and I don't expect to see him in the starting line-up either, but I do expect a performance that underlines our tremendous season. All the players will be fit for this one, that's a definite; nobody wants to miss out on an appearance at Old Trafford. I remember once Leeds fans singing at us that this was 'Swansea's cup final', to play Leeds United. I found this quite amusing, because it wasn't, in fact. The last time I heard that on a battle-weary day in Leeds I laughed. How deluded can you be? However, this is a cup final of sorts, to play at Old Trafford is a great feeling for players, clubs and fans alike. I have seen the Swans here before in a far more turbulent time when we went down 1–0 during our first season in the old top division. That was the season when Manchester United were easily beaten at the Vetch Field, along with Arsenal, Manchester City, Liverpool and all. This season has been similar – full of excitement and hope – but this time around things feel very different. Yes we may be in times of austerity, or so I am told by those who control us (but you don't have my mind), but back then there was more of an edge. Whether that was my youth or immaturity I am not sure, but it felt different.

I settle down in front of the TV with a cold beer (limiting my intake these days for special occasions and days that are either midweek days, or weekends or start with an M, T, W, F or S). It's quite a build-up with little or, maybe more accurately, nothing said about Swansea City because this day is all about how many goals Manchester United must score to beat us and gain ground in the goal difference stakes on their near neighbours City. With only one game on the Saturday, a 3–3 draw between a lacklustre Norwich and moaning Arsenal, we have a full compliment of games today with Blackburn and Wigan thrashing it out to avoid relegation on Monday. Another exciting game to watch I am sure. City beat Newcastle 2–0 and that is the big focus – with one exception. As predicted QPR get three points to take them into the last game of the season with a glimmer of hope and a fourth-from-bottom spot. I just feel they will make it and if Wigan get the points at Blackburn and send them down they too may well be ready again for a spot of the Houdini magic. Some will say they are already safe after demolishing Newcastle 4–0 a few days ago. What an incredible turnaround.

The country's fixation with the big clubs in the Premier League goes on and on as the afternoon progresses to kick-off. Very little is said at all about our magnificent team and wonderful season; it's all red and all Manchester United. What can be guaranteed is that I will not be in front of any TV next weekend – I have had enough of this bias already. No matter what happens today, and I have to be honest we are stone-cold losers in most people's minds, the real winners are the superb away support at Old Trafford. The Jack Army is in fine voice and their voices crush the Old Trafford faithful who are in excess of 70,000. A remarkable confirmation that this side's fans expect results, or perhaps they already know that City have the title all sewn up?

The game itself went pretty much as I expected with United making the most of their chances and the Swans not taking theirs. A shame maybe, but the 2–0 scoreline and three points for United was in no way a shock. For me, I didn't want a thrashing – many teams have been here before and fallen down by as many as eight goals this season (that team was Arsenal). That was never going to happen to us, and if we had taken our chances we may well have had a share of the spoils. United were eight points clear of City four weeks ago and now they go in to the last game of the season having to win and hope QPR of all teams do them a favour at the Etihad. An improbable scenario.

The Swans had nine shots on target and Danny Graham should have scored easily in the second half and maybe Gylfi too, but overall we left the game as we started, with our dignity intact and our credentials very much endorsed as a good, well-shaped and tactically aware Premier League club. No fears there. The media bias (oh, havent I mentioned them recently?) was evident in the match reports after the game. The BBC website didn't mention one of the Swansea opportunities whatsoever and concentrated on a completely biased and ill-informed report on Manchester United – no other team mattered. Judging by his report, BBC journalist Alistair Magowan ought to be ashamed of himself, and if it's not him then his editor should be. Sky did equally as poorly and I get the feeling that many fans who have been here before me must get that self-same feeling. When the chips are down, the top four matter most, and in particular the rich clubs and richer owners get the headlines, and as we at Swansea can offer them nothing, nothing is what we get. The Swans remain in twelfth spot on forty-four points and the bottom three reflect Wolves (down) and Blackburn (as good as down) and Bolton. All need to win their remaining games and even then they may well be relegated, such is the formality of the season at this time of the year.

The next night Blackburn are sent down (with an accompanying protest against Steve Kean), Wigan winning 1–0 and securing their future once more in the Premier League. Their recent form is that of champions, not relegation fodder. A top-ten finish would still be achieved if all the results went our way and the Swans beat Liverpool – another doubtful prospect if the experts are to be believed. However, this is the last game of the season and anything can happen. Talk turns to how many millions can be gained and lost for winning one game and increasing the club's finishing position. It is astounding but true that millions and millions of pounds actually do depend on this.

Quite simply, clubs have three main revenue streams: match day income (from tickets, corporate dining and promotions), media income and commercial income – things like kit deals, sponsorship, merchandise, tours and so on. It's a minefield of opportunity for Premier League clubs. The Premier League winners will earn £60,602,289. Swansea get £13,788,093 in UK TV revenue and £18,764,644 in foreign TV revenue. And that's not all. The games we played at home saw us gain £485,000 per live TV match plus money for web, phone and delayed rights too. An incredible sum alone. But let's move on – Swansea City earn just under £46m for the season and each Premier League place is worth £755,062. That sum goes to the bottom club and every place earned after that earns the same – £755,062. These are exact facts and figures, so please don't think in any way that I am having a stab in the dark. Blackpool, West Ham and Birmingham all had parachute payments of £15,475,005 to boot. I am not surprised they all featured at the top end of their league at the end of April. Did you know that Portsmouth also got just over £12m in revenue from the Premier League in the 2011/12 season? Well you do now – as did Hull and Burnley. All these clubs are distant Premier League memories, but their bank balances are very healthy. Middlesbrough got over £4m! In fact Swansea City earn more from Premier League central funds and facility fees – their first premier league season – than Stoke, Wigan, Aston Villa, Blackburn, Bolton, Norwich, QPR, Sunderland, WBA and Wolves. This is not debatable, it is pure financial fact. Add to that the fact that Aston Villa pay an average player fee of £2.5m a year and are the forty-first best-payers of sports stars (not just football, I mean all sports) in the world! They need success more than most.

Swansea is a club that ten years ago went for a £1 to a group of local businessmen, a South African and a Dutchman from The Hague, and that is now one of the richest in world football. So do I feel bad about not taking my interest further when given the opportunity back in 2002? Not at all – they each deserve to be a part of what they made, and nobody should feel any moment of jealousy as a result. I am sure the board members are well versed in these matters, and whatever financial rewards they have they can justify every time you and I look at the Premier League table.

So we are here, at the very end of a season that has given us all so much. The end of a ten-year period that has seen the club rise to be the richest, best-placed and best club side in Wales; it is beyond any doubt at all. Further east they are green-eyed as they stuttered towards another play-off and then fell apart as they were hammered by West Ham – not only hammered, in fact they were battered and embarrassed. By the time the final is played we at Swansea will have our feet up at home, cigar (or electronic cigarette well lit) and a quick shot of celebratory brandy poured. We have one more game to play. And if you review those figures you will know that any sort of win will earn the club potentially millions in prize money.

Liverpool will want a bit of this as they officially pay an average (per player) wage of £60k a week at Anfield – that is an average per-player wage of over £3m a year. These levels of cash must make you very comfortable indeed, but it is beyond any comparison I can make in any stratosphere I can relate to. It's just amazing, and somewhat taints any love I have for the game.

As the sell-out crowd heads to the Liberty these figures are discussed – some get it very wrong. I know the figures, I have to because I am going to tell all you lot about them, so they have to be exact. But the reasoning is the same, we need to win this and end the season as we started it, a complete and respected Premier League team. The crowd trail down the hilly roads and carriageways with one mission – click, click – to the Liberty Stadium and the hallowed turf and hallowed ground of Swansea. The Scousers are here. The perms have gone, as have the 'taches, but look at the Swansea City side of '81 and you will see very similar haircuts and poses.

In opposition are little Swansea, lucky first-season wonders, the club with second-season syndrome written all over them. A club that at the start of the season had just one man – Scott Sinclair – and progressed slowly to an admirable eleven by this game. The players now are known, and not laughed at as bystanders in the Sinclair show. Scott has had some wonderful moments this season and maybe by the end of next he will be the complete player, the real deal if his fitness regimes continue . . . only time will tell. The murmurings of England inclusion were never going to happen, like Nathan Dyer and Leon Briton – all were talked about as England hopefuls, but they would never feature, not as long as the English influence wore blinkers. The country's desire to fail is confirmed the minute they pick players who are out of touch, out of sight and out to grass. You have to laugh.

The chanting rises over our heads and the sun shines on this glorious May day. Some folk wear shorts in the hope that if they do it will get warmer – it won't though, this is a cold May remember. Stalls outside the ground sell things none of us want, the club shop has a sale on and is ready for the next Premier League lorryfull of stock that sees our commercial turnover increase again and again. The pubs spill out drunk men and shouting ladies, none of whom I recall at Hartlepool when Andy Cook broke his leg, but as welcome I suppose as any Swans supporter, they all have their place. They all want a piece of this action. The drink will cloud their view and in some cases prevent any view of the game at all. Entry (and lawful entry at that) to any football ground has to be a considered approach if you have take on board more fuel than a Boeing 747.

I have made the journey from Gloucester (best tourist destination 1991, yes, 1991), as have the rest of our happy band. Jon, Andy, Howard and co are all happy and content that a Globe Sunday lunch and a beer or two is sufficient to balance our minds before the prized players of Liverpool face off against our brave team in white with flashes of brilliance. The crowd is assembled and the roar begins. 'Hymns and Arias' is sung and the 'Vetch Field way down by the sea' is referred to. Swansea, oh Swansea! Today you have my heart and soul, and no matter the occasion you will always have these things so precious to me. Our journey ends today so let's make it a winning end to a fantastic season that many said we would never compete in. The London hacks, precious in their ignorance of facts, arrogant in their misguided and foolish stance against this valiant side now talk of second-season failings. You fools – you know nothing. But then you never did.

The Welsh media want some of this as well; they now realise that they have no choice but to say Swansea first in news reports. You can't keep mentioning the worst team first when the best is staring straight in your face. We all know now who is best at everything, and every week that is reinforced. So I reinforce it again, here and now. A packed ground and celebration is on the menu, pure celebration of our sporting achievement, heritage and belief.

John Roder is seen sneaking into the ground, his voice a distinguished and comforting sound for any matchday commentary – he knows his way round here now does John. Dalglish is seen as well – a shadow of what he was way back when he was a legend to some. Today he is twisted, confused and constantly frowning. He seems tormented and distracted; maybe he knows more about his destiny than he wishes to say? I am reliably informed he will be summoned to the USA come midweek, and there the club's owners, the Fenway Sports Group, will speak with a man who finds it difficult to accept he is wrong or see the effect he has on the bigger picture. If you want my personal opinion (well, you're going to have it anyway), this Kenny Dalglish is walking a tightrope, and it is about to snap. The brand of the Red Sox and the brand of the future is not evident in a craggy-featured man approaching the twilight of his life who is best retired and put away to a quieter place.

The scene is set and the half starts as we expect with a Swan flying and a Liver bird dying. Oh, the prose it knows no bounds my friends. Gylfi has a few chances and Leon torments again as Dyer presents some real issues for the Liverpool defence. Today it's Vorm with Williams, Taylor, Caulker and Rangel at the back – our first-choice back four. In midfield are Britton, Sinclair, Dyer, Allen and Sigurdsson, so the supply valve is very much open. Up front is Danny Graham in search of his hundredth career goal.

Liverpool look in disarray at times, poorly managed on the field with little answer to the onslaught from Swansea City. For all our efforts, though, the half finishes at 0–0. Liverpool players walk from the pitch ready for a Scotsman's interpretation on a Welsh pitch in an English league, while a Northern Irishman will dissect his own team's efforts for fifteen cool minutes.

As Kevin Johns shouts just one more time at Cyril, and a young boy takes a long run-up to shoot and score, the break is time for me to reflect in a quiet moment at the foot of the East Stand, Swansea. Our own east side, our own cavern of noise. I could never have believed it had you said to me back in May 2011, as I fell and found myself down and out in my garden, that this would be our season's end. Secure and safe, and playing Liverpool at home in a match that rewards us only with more money. Personally I feel OK, and this is a good feeling all told, my only worry is this book and all that it holds and what it means to you, and the many thousands it will reach and hopefully touch in the future.

I am cold and shiver, I look up to the back of the stand and see the chaps assembled there as ever; Carl and Mick, Tom, Ian Blackmore and the Gloucester few, Phil, Ian and John – others too who I cannot recall knowing that well but who talk to me anyway. Hello Nigel Drean! I see you too mate, wearing an Elvis Costello mask, in contravention of the required Elvis code for today. This is Swansea in 2012, and those who haven't been so lucky as to witness these recent events; the long-gone or -lost Jacks of old deserve a thought today as well. They may be gone, but are not forgotten by those who hold them dear. The teams come out and the final throes of a season unfurl before us.

Both sides are evenly matched and it's Liverpool who at last show some competency on the turf as Maxi plays his part as does Carroll, Henderson and Kelly – and Carragher, too – an aggressive man who is clearly off the pace and making up for it with a feisty tackle or two. Mistimed and miscalculated aggression, I am afraid. Rangel starts to combine with Sinclair and they both look far more comfortable when both are on the field, Rangel supporting Scott and supplying a pass he willingly takes. The cross is precise and is met by Danny Graham who fires his shot coolly in to the back of the net. The ground erupts, the celebrations begin and thousands of Elvis Presleys (and one Elvis Costello) join in the cheer. It's the winning goal of course, and Brendan salutes his troops as the Liverpool attack fires blanks. Swansea cope admirably with all that is thrown at them. The score is 1–0 as Mark Halsey brings matters to an end after five minutes of added time. The players are applauded from the pitch by 20,000 folk all happy at the victory and the prospect of another Premier League season. The PA system asks for no fan invasions of the pitch and a naked man runs westwards. Then the players return, they have family with them, babies and kids, wives and girlfriends. I'm not sure if I care, but some do. I leave the ground. Brendan waves and his wife waves too. Is this the new royal family?

Our car radio talks about the most memorable season on record as Manchester City secured the Premier League title with the last kick of their game against QPR. Bolton failed to get a good enough result at Stoke and are relegated. The Rs are still a Premier League club. Oh dear, still – so are we and that is what matters. Swansea achieve an eleventh-place finish, while Wolves are twentieth (you work out the winnings). I work out the cost as do many other fans and supporters of our club. Financially, well, we have been here before, but emotionally it's hard to gauge. All I know is that there were emotions and there were many. I have given my heart and soul to my team, and most of the time they have given it back. This is our agreement, our gentleman's agreement while they wear our club's shirt. It's been bloody good so I thank you all. And now as the season ends, I look forward to a quiet summer and time to pause.

I have never been one to keep quiet when a noise needed to be made, and I have also remained quiet when there was a need to say something, anything in a moment that demanded a word or two. I hope this journey was to your liking. If the reviews and letters, mails and texts from the last effort are anything to go by then this will be well received. From an historical point of view it is a document that is there for all to enjoy for many years to come, probably long after me and thee have departed on that last football special to wherever that train ends up. The toil and trouble following our team is nothing compared to the lives of many that have real problems and issues to deal with and manage every day. This is merely a football book, a biographical account from someone with too much time on their hands and too little time to fulfill the ambition others had for me. I finish here at the end of the 2011/12 season having bared my inner self all over these pages and leave you, I hope, in some spirit if not a little hope. In another year I feel there won't be another book for you to peruse and disagree with, laugh at and argue with me about. I need a rest, and a long one at that. Permanently resigning myself to the fact that this is my last effort in a series of efforts over the years.

Of course, once refreshed you never know, but writing a book takes a huge chunk out of your spirit and saps you to the core. It doesn't irritate but there is never any replenishment or refuelling and the state it leaves you in at the end is the state you are in for the rest of your life. This much I do know – this book has left me drained but happy, accomplished and fulfilled. Like our club I leave you now, happy, content and a winner. The best of the rest and maybe better than that? Swansea City may well have other scalps to take and other dreams to make real, and I hope above all else we are all there to watch it and relish every moment.

There has to be an end and for this book this is my end, and for you my friend, another chapter is finished. Our end is complete and we have completed it together.

Forward into Battle.

And so the Journey Begins Again

I really thought this would be it – the end of my scribblings for a while – then the telephone rings, and the football world that refuses to sleep is at it again. 'Brendan Rodgers is going to Liverpool,' I am told. I immediately laugh it off telling my caller that he turned that nugget down two weeks back when Dalglish was sacked. I am then told that he has changed tack and is ready to sign on the dotted line and the country will wake in the morning to the news that this is a real story and a real goer. Brendan is not rumoured to be going to Liverpool, he has gone, and all that is left is for the financial clause in his contract to be activated and Swansea get £5m in compensation. It seemed to me that the Liverpool owners had seen and heard enough of not only Dalglish to sack him, but of Brendan as well to want to employ him. I don't blame them at all – we have already talked about his qualities and ability to represent a brand as well as the club, coach and players. He is a diamond. He takes with him Colin Pascoe as well, and I wish him well too, in that Liverpool dressing room. Brendan will need all the support he can get.

I genuinely thought Brendan would stay around for another season, but I am not that bothered; we have been here before, and no doubt this will happen again. The Swansea ship is infested with rats – the rats of other clubs, that is. The lazy clubs who come fishing every time we unveil a new player or manager. It seems they like our style, and this is to be embraced. We are not doing too badly as a result either. There are now fans who are forlorn but that is their problem; I've said this before – worship these people and you have to be prepared to be upset when these things happen. Remember this club and its colours and characters is on loan from us – the fans. We remain, while they all come and go. Get used to it.

The more successful we are, the more things like this will happen. Consider it an endorsement as to what we do, and how we do it. So now we have a new manager in Michael Laudrup and we wish him well as he puts on the shoes of Martinez, Rodgers and to an extent Sousa too. He has much to prove and much to show and as a busy Premier League season is again on the horizon, I can only wish him all the best. Make a success of it and well, you never know where you will end up. This is yet another Swansea journey about to get underway, and one which we will all be watching closely. I have to, I am a Swansea City supporter and a proud one at that – like all things the players, managers and most staff all come and go, but we are the remaining constant, the relied-upon that is forever Swansea, forever true. Our integrity always intact. We are the true Swansea spirit.

And so it all starts again. Same club, same voices, same passion. Laudrup is already instilling confidence in all the supporters for the season to come. The rivalry continues across the South Wales divide, be it in pubs, clubs, work places or, indeed, at an obscure race meeting in Berkshire. Laudrup has all this to take on board including the significance of the task that is ahead of him, his staff and, indeed, his family.

Michael is now Laudrup SA1, and for me he is the new wave, the new breed and the new way. Something tells me that we are now again in a new era, and that era is going to be one hell of a rock 'n' roll party.

Tune 'em up, the main stage awaits us all.

Keith Haynes, July 2012

Also by Keith Haynes

Come on Cymru, 1999
Come on Cymru, 2000
Vetch Field Voices (reprinted and updated), 2011
100 Swansea Greats (reprinted and updated), 2011
Another Day at the Office: Roger Freestone, 2002
The Tony Ford Story, 2005
Gloucester: Photographic Memories, 2007
Swansea City 2010/11: Walking on Sunshine, 2011